CW01620118

COURAGE

The 7 minute journal for gratitude, healing & empowerment

First published November 2024 by Paradisium Publishing

Copyright (c) Linzi Meaden 2024

ISBN: 978-1-9168778-2-5

All rights reserved. No part of this publication may be reproduced, stored or transmitted in any form or by any means, electronic, mechanical, photocopying, recording, scanning or otherwise without written permission from the publisher or creator.

The intent of the creator of this journal is to provide general guidance and support to improve your emotional, mental and spiritual well-being. If you choose to use any of the information, the creator and publisher cannot be held responsible for your actions.

This journal is not a replacement for therapy or medical advice.

Created by Linzi Meaden
Trauma Therapist and
Mental Health Advocate

Visit
linzimeaden.com

courage

write a new beginning

how to get the most out of this journal, made just for you

Welcome to your journal - your portal to new beginnings, self-discovery, personal growth and the limitless possibilities that await within.

We all have our own stories that are holding us back, but how many of us take action to change them, to re-write them and become the person we desire?

There's a reason you are reading this; you are already taking action and for this I personally want to celebrate YOU!

You have a mission, a purpose. You have COURAGE.

As you explore these pages, allow your thoughts, emotions and feelings to flow freely, create your desires, take action, and ultimately by changing your story,
you are changing your life, one page at a time.

Thank you for being You

Linzi x

Here you will find your daily journal pages; one for morning and one for evening.

You will also find some additional pages appearing throughout the journal with words of wisdom, beautiful poems and space for your own reflections / ideas / inspirations.

Place your journal next to your bed with your favourite pen so it's always within easy reach. Better still, move any distractions, e.g., your smartphone (if you use one) to the other side of the room - or another room altogether!

Write in your journal as soon as you wake up and before you go to sleep. It's as simple as that and this is where the magic happens.

The first moments after your wake shape the rest of your day. Even if you have excuses for not having the time or wanting to write today, just write it anyway. It only takes a few minutes.

Consistency is key. Expression heals where suppression destroys. There will be some resistance. Remember why you are doing this as this will keep you motivated on days when you feel like giving up.

Remember: we are what we repeatedly do. Writing in your journal everyday will become a beautiful habit where you'll be richly rewarded.

My Purpose
My Mission

My Agreement /Commitment To Myself

My Soundtrack

Music feeds the soul
Music changes our mood
Music helps us to get up and move or
Slow down and relax.
Music makes the difference

Add these tracks to a playlist: listen at home, exercising, driving, cooking, working, anytime!

My upbeat / happy / energising tunes & songs

My soothing, peaceful, nurturing tunes & songs

When you declutter your mind & body, it's also good to declutter your environment...

Your environment is important too, especially when you are investing in your mental wellbeing / mind health.

Your Home / Space:

Do a 'spring clean' now, regardless of what season we are in.

Move items / furniture around.

Change or add art / prints / photographs.

Clear out drawers and cupboards.

Move items that have been in the same place for months/years/decades! You'll be amazed out how this can make you feel.

Clear out books / paperwork.

Donate to charity or local communities wherever possible.

And it's not just tangible things...... a 'spring clean' of your relationships / friendships may benefit you too!

The Humble Wood

The sun bravely bares its way through the
awning of leaves above me.

Little parcels of light,
keeping watch on me as I go.

The earthly scent gently seeps into my nose;
I am no longer an intruder
but part of this vibrant world that
reaches out to me so firmly.

Those sweet singers begin
their mellow chorale.
Nothing is to see, but all is to hear.

So lilting is the tune,
That I can only but,
bathe myself in their harmony.

Poem by
Deirdre Whitmore

© copyright Deirdre Whitmore 2024

Courageous Hearts & Brave Voices

MORNING REFLECTION

My Power Word: " " Date:..................

Hmmm.... How I Feel Right Now Great

0 1 2 3 4 5 6 7 8 9 10

Today I'm grateful for:

My intention for the day:

A belief / habit to change:

What I can do today to get me closer to where I want to be tomorrow:

My daily affirmation:

EVENING REFLECTION

Date:..................

How I Feel Before Sleep

Hmmm.... Peaceful / Grateful

0 1 2 3 4 5 6 7 8 9 10

What did I learn today?

....

....

....

How I showed or received kindness today (others/self):

....

....

....

How I connected with nature today:

....

....

....

Something I did or said which took courage:

....

....

....

Who (which part of me) will show up tomorrow to make the day even better?

Creator / Magician ☐ ....

Warrior / Courage ☐ ....

Leader / Inspiration ☐ ....

Love / Authentic Self ☐

MORNING REFLECTION

My Power Word: "   "Date:..................

Hmmm....   How I Feel Right Now   Great

0 1 2 3 4 5 6 7 8 9 10

Today I'm grateful for:

....

....

....

My intention for the day:

....

....

....

A belief / habit to change:

....

....

....

What I can do today to get me closer to where I want to be tomorrow:

....

....

....

My daily affirmation:

....

....

....

EVENING REFLECTION

Date:..................

How I Feel Before Sleep

Hmmm.... Peaceful / Grateful

0 1 2 3 4 5 6 7 8 9 10

What did I learn today?

....

....

....

How I showed or received kindness today (others/self):

....

....

....

How I connected with nature today:

....

....

....

Something I did or said which took courage:

....

....

....

Who (which part of me) will show up tomorrow to make the day even better?

- [ ] Creator / Magician
- [ ] Warrior / Courage
- [ ] Leader / Inspiration
- [ ] Love / Authentic Self

....

....

....

MORNING REFLECTION

My Power Word: " "Date:..................

Hmmm.... **How I Feel Right Now** Great

0 1 2 3 4 5 6 7 8 9 10

Today I'm grateful for:

My intention for the day:

A belief / habit to change:

What I can do today to get me closer to where I want to be tomorrow:

My daily affirmation:

EVENING REFLECTION

Date:..................

How I Feel Before Sleep

Hmmm.... Peaceful / Grateful

0 1 2 3 4 5 6 7 8 9 10

What did I learn today?

....

....

....

How I showed or received kindness today (others/self):

....

....

....

How I connected with nature today:

....

....

....

Something I did or said which took courage:

....

....

....

Who (which part of me) will show up tomorrow to make the day even better?

- Creator / Magician ☐
- Warrior / Courage ☐
- Leader / Inspiration ☐
- Love / Authentic Self ☐

....

....

....

MORNING REFLECTION

My Power Word: " " Date:.................

Hmmm.... How I Feel Right Now Great

0 1 2 3 4 5 6 7 8 9 10

Today I'm grateful for:

My intention for the day:

A belief / habit to change:

What I can do today to get me closer to where I want to be tomorrow:

My daily affirmation:

EVENING REFLECTION

Date:..................

How I Feel Before Sleep

Hmmm... Peaceful / Grateful

0 1 2 3 4 5 6 7 8 9 10

What did I learn today?

....

....

....

How I showed or received kindness today (others/self):

....

....

....

How I connected with nature today:

....

....

....

Something I did or said which took courage:

....

....

....

Who (which part of me) will show up tomorrow to make the day even better?

Creator / Magician ☐

Warrior / Courage ☐

Leader / Inspiration ☐

Love / Authentic Self ☐

....

....

....

MORNING REFLECTION

My Power Word: " "Date:................

Hmmm.... **How I Feel Right Now** Great

0 1 2 3 4 5 6 7 8 9 10

Today I'm grateful for:

....

....

....

My intention for the day:

....

....

....

A belief / habit to change:

....

....

....

What I can do today to get me closer to where I want to be tomorrow:

....

....

....

My daily affirmation:

....

....

....

EVENING REFLECTION

Date:..................

How I Feel Before Sleep

Hmmm.... Peaceful / Grateful

0 1 2 3 4 5 6 7 8 9 10

What did I learn today?

How I showed or received kindness today (others/self):

How I connected with nature today:

Something I did or said which took courage:

Who (which part of me) will show up tomorrow to make the day even better?

Creator / Magician

Warrior / Courage

Leader / Inspiration

Love / Authentic Self

practise gratitude daily… and you'll have more to be grateful for

MORNING REFLECTION

My Power Word: "   **" Date:..................**

Hmmm....   **How I Feel Right Now**   Great

0 1 2 3 4 5 6 7 8 9 10

Today I'm grateful for:

....

....

....

My intention for the day:

....

....

....

A belief / habit to change:

....

....

....

What I can do today to get me closer to where I want to be tomorrow:

....

....

....

My daily affirmation:

....

....

....

EVENING REFLECTION

Date:..................

How I Feel Before Sleep

Hmmm.... Peaceful / Grateful

0 1 2 3 4 5 6 7 8 9 10

What did I learn today?

....

....

....

How I showed or received kindness today (others/self):

....

....

....

How I connected with nature today:

....

....

....

Something I did or said which took courage:

....

....

....

Who (which part of me) will show up tomorrow to make the day even better?

Creator / Magician ☐ ....

Warrior / Courage ☐ ....

Leader / Inspiration ☐ ....

Love / Authentic Self ☐

MORNING REFLECTION

My Power Word: "   " Date:..................

Hmmm.... **How I Feel Right Now** Great

0 1 2 3 4 5 6 7 8 9 10

Today I'm grateful for:

My intention for the day:

A belief / habit to change:

What I can do today to get me closer to where I want to be tomorrow:

My daily affirmation:

EVENING REFLECTION

Date:..................

How I Feel Before Sleep

Hmmm.... Peaceful / Grateful

0 1 2 3 4 5 6 7 8 9 10

What did I learn today?

....

....

....

How I showed or received kindness today (others/self):

....

....

....

How I connected with nature today:

....

....

....

Something I did or said which took courage:

....

....

....

Who (which part of me) will show up tomorrow to make the day even better?

Creator / Magician ☐

Warrior / Courage ☐

Leader / Inspiration ☐

Love / Authentic Self ☐

....

....

....

MORNING REFLECTION

My Power Word: "   "Date:.................

Hmmm....   How I Feel Right Now   Great

0 1 2 3 4 5 6 7 8 9 10

Today I'm grateful for:

....

....

....

My intention for the day:

....

....

....

A belief / habit to change:

....

....

....

What I can do today to get me closer to where I want to be tomorrow:

....

....

....

My daily affirmation:

....

....

....

EVENING REFLECTION

Date:..................

How I Feel Before Sleep

Hmmm.... Peaceful / Grateful

0 1 2 3 4 5 6 7 8 9 10

What did I learn today?

....

....

....

How I showed or received kindness today (others/self):

....

....

....

How I connected with nature today:

....

....

....

Something I did or said which took courage:

....

....

....

Who (which part of me) will show up tomorrow to make the day even better?

- [ ] Creator / Magician
- [ ] Warrior / Courage
- [ ] Leader / Inspiration
- [ ] Love / Authentic Self

....

....

....

Creating A New Positive Habit Starts Now, Right Now, This Moment...

MORNING REFLECTION

My Power Word: " "Date:.................

Hmmm.... How I Feel Right Now Great

0 1 2 3 4 5 6 7 8 9 10

Today I'm grateful for:

My intention for the day:

A belief / habit to change:

What I can do today to get me closer to where I want to be tomorrow:

My daily affirmation:

EVENING REFLECTION

Date:..................

How I Feel Before Sleep

Hmmm.... Peaceful / Grateful

0 1 2 3 4 5 6 7 8 9 10

What did I learn today?

How I showed or received kindness today (others/self):

How I connected with nature today:

Something I did or said which took courage:

Who (which part of me) will show up tomorrow to make the day even better?

- Creator / Magician ☐
- Warrior / Courage ☐
- Leader / Inspiration ☐
- Love / Authentic Self ☐

MORNING REFLECTION

My Power Word: " "Date:.................

Hmmm.... How I Feel Right Now Great

0 1 2 3 4 5 6 7 8 9 10

Today I'm grateful for:

....

....

....

My intention for the day:

....

....

....

A belief / habit to change:

....

....

....

What I can do today to get me closer to where I want to be tomorrow:

....

....

....

My daily affirmation:

....

....

....

EVENING REFLECTION

Date:..................

How I Feel Before Sleep

Hmmm.... Peaceful / Grateful

0 1 2 3 4 5 6 7 8 9 10

What did I learn today?

How I showed or received kindness today (others/self):

How I connected with nature today:

Something I did or said which took courage:

Who (which part of me) will show up tomorrow to make the day even better?

Creator / Magician ☐

Warrior / Courage ☐

Leader / Inspiration ☐

Love / Authentic Self ☐

MORNING REFLECTION

My Power Word: "   " Date:..................

Hmmm.... **How I Feel Right Now** Great

0 1 2 3 4 5 6 7 8 9 10

Today I'm grateful for:

My intention for the day:

A belief / habit to change:

What I can do today to get me closer to where I want to be tomorrow:

My daily affirmation:

EVENING REFLECTION

Date:..................

How I Feel Before Sleep

Hmmm.... Peaceful / Grateful

0 1 2 3 4 5 6 7 8 9 10

What did I learn today?

....

....

....

How I showed or received kindness today (others/self):

....

....

....

How I connected with nature today:

....

....

....

Something I did or said which took courage:

....

....

....

Who (which part of me) will show up tomorrow to make the day even better?

Creator / Magician ☐

Warrior / Courage ☐

Leader / Inspiration ☐

Love / Authentic Self ☐

....

....

....

MORNING REFLECTION

My Power Word: "   " Date:..................

Hmmm....   How I Feel Right Now   Great

0 1 2 3 4 5 6 7 8 9 10

Today I'm grateful for:

....

....

....

My intention for the day:

....

....

....

A belief / habit to change:

....

....

....

What I can do today to get me closer to where I want to be tomorrow:

....

....

....

My daily affirmation:

....

....

....

EVENING REFLECTION

Date:..................

How I Feel Before Sleep

Hmmm.... Peaceful / Grateful

0 1 2 3 4 5 6 7 8 9 10

What did I learn today?

How I showed or received kindness today (others/self):

How I connected with nature today:

Something I did or said which took courage:

Who (which part of me) will show up tomorrow to make the day even better?

- Creator / Magician
- Warrior / Courage
- Leader / Inspiration
- Love / Authentic Self

MORNING REFLECTION

My Power Word: "   " Date:..................

Hmmm.... How I Feel Right Now Great

0 1 2 3 4 5 6 7 8 9 10

Today I'm grateful for:

....

....

....

My intention for the day:

....

....

....

A belief / habit to change:

....

....

....

What I can do today to get me closer to where I want to be tomorrow:

....

....

....

My daily affirmation:

....

....

....

EVENING REFLECTION

Date:.................

How I Feel Before Sleep

Hmmm.... Peaceful / Grateful

0 1 2 3 4 5 6 7 8 9 10

What did I learn today?

....

....

....

How I showed or received kindness today (others/self):

....

....

....

How I connected with nature today:

....

....

....

Something I did or said which took courage:

....

....

....

Who (which part of me) will show up tomorrow to make the day even better?

- Creator / Magician ☐ ....
- Warrior / Courage ☐ ....
- Leader / Inspiration ☐ ....
- Love / Authentic Self ☐

bonus day

My Power Word: Date:

Mood/Emotion Tracker

○ ○ ○ ○ ○

SAD / LOW ⟷ HAPPY / ENERGISED

I am Grateful for:

My Intention / Focus for today:

Space for Creativity

DOODLE, COLOUR, WORDS, THOUGHTS

My Purpose / Mission:

What I GET to do today:

MORNING REFLECTION

My Power Word: " "Date:..................

Hmmm.... How I Feel Right Now Great

0 1 2 3 4 5 6 7 8 9 10

Today I'm grateful for:

My intention for the day:

A belief / habit to change:

What I can do today to get me closer to where I want to be tomorrow:

My daily affirmation:

EVENING REFLECTION

Date:.................

How I Feel Before Sleep

Hmmm.... Peaceful / Grateful

0 1 2 3 4 5 6 7 8 9 10

What did I learn today?

How I showed or received kindness today (others/self):

How I connected with nature today:

Something I did or said which took courage:

Who (which part of me) will show up tomorrow to make the day even better?

- Creator / Magician ☐
- Warrior / Courage ☐
- Leader / Inspiration ☐
- Love / Authentic Self ☐

MORNING REFLECTION

My Power Word: "　　　　　　　　　　" Date:..................

Hmmm.... How I Feel Right Now Great

0 1 2 3 4 5 6 7 8 9 10

Today I'm grateful for:

My intention for the day:

A belief / habit to change:

What I can do today to get me closer to where I want to be tomorrow:

My daily affirmation:

EVENING REFLECTION

Date:.................

How I Feel Before Sleep

Hmmm.... Peaceful / Grateful

0 1 2 3 4 5 6 7 8 9 10

What did I learn today?

....

....

....

How I showed or received kindness today (others/self):

....

....

....

How I connected with nature today:

....

....

....

Something I did or said which took courage:

....

....

....

Who (which part of me) will show up tomorrow to make the day even better?

- Creator / Magician ☐
- Warrior / Courage ☐
- Leader / Inspiration ☐
- Love / Authentic Self ☐

....

....

....

MORNING REFLECTION

My Power Word: " "Date:.................

Hmmm.... How I Feel Right Now Great

0 1 2 3 4 5 6 7 8 9 10

Today I'm grateful for:

....

....

....

My intention for the day:

....

....

....

A belief / habit to change:

....

....

....

What I can do today to get me closer to where I want to be tomorrow:

....

....

....

My daily affirmation:

....

....

....

EVENING REFLECTION

Date:..................

How I Feel Before Sleep

Hmmm.... Peaceful / Grateful

0 1 2 3 4 5 6 7 8 9 10

What did I learn today?

How I showed or received kindness today (others/self):

How I connected with nature today:

Something I did or said which took courage:

Who (which part of me) will show up tomorrow to make the day even better?

- Creator / Magician
- Warrior / Courage
- Leader / Inspiration
- Love / Authentic Self

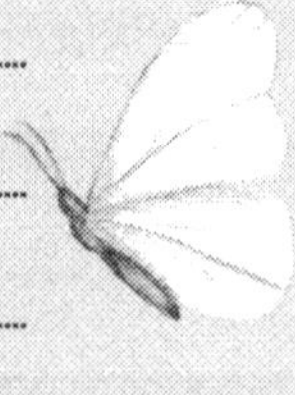

MORNING REFLECTION

My Power Word: " "Date:.................

Hmmm.... How I Feel Right Now Great

0 1 2 3 4 5 6 7 8 9 10

Today I'm grateful for:

....

....

....

My intention for the day:

....

....

....

A belief / habit to change:

....

....

....

What I can do today to get me closer to where I want to be tomorrow:

....

....

....

My daily affirmation:

....

....

....

EVENING REFLECTION

Date:..................

How I Feel Before Sleep

Hmmm.... Peaceful / Grateful

0 1 2 3 4 5 6 7 8 9 10

What did I learn today?

....

....

....

How I showed or received kindness today (others/self):

....

....

....

How I connected with nature today:

....

....

....

Something I did or said which took courage:

....

....

....

Who (which part of me) will show up tomorrow to make the day even better?

- Creator / Magician ☐
- Warrior / Courage ☐
- Leader / Inspiration ☐
- Love / Authentic Self ☐

....

....

....

BREATHE IN

CONFIDENCE

BREATHE OUT

DOUBT

MORNING REFLECTION

My Power Word: " "Date:.................

Hmmm.... How I Feel Right Now Great

0 1 2 3 4 5 6 7 8 9 10

Today I'm grateful for:

My intention for the day:

A belief / habit to change:

What I can do today to get me closer to where I want to be tomorrow:

My daily affirmation:

EVENING REFLECTION

Date:..................

How I Feel Before Sleep

Hmmm.... Peaceful / Grateful

0 1 2 3 4 5 6 7 8 9 10

What did I learn today?

How I showed or received kindness today (others/self):

How I connected with nature today:

Something I did or said which took courage:

Who (which part of me) will show up tomorrow to make the day even better?

- Creator / Magician ☐
- Warrior / Courage ☐
- Leader / Inspiration ☐
- Love / Authentic Self ☐

MORNING REFLECTION

My Power Word: "   "Date:.................

Hmmm.... **How I Feel Right Now** Great

0 1 2 3 4 5 6 7 8 9 10

Today I'm grateful for:

My intention for the day:

A belief / habit to change:

What I can do today to get me closer to where I want to be tomorrow:

My daily affirmation:

EVENING REFLECTION

Date:..................

How I Feel Before Sleep

Hmmm.... Peaceful / Grateful

0 1 2 3 4 5 6 7 8 9 10

What did I learn today?

How I showed or received kindness today (others/self):

How I connected with nature today:

Something I did or said which took courage:

Who (which part of me) will show up tomorrow to make the day even better?

- Creator / Magician
- Warrior / Courage
- Leader / Inspiration
- Love / Authentic Self

MORNING REFLECTION

My Power Word: " " Date:.................

Hmmm.... How I Feel Right Now Great

0 1 2 3 4 5 6 7 8 9 10

Today I'm grateful for:

....

....

....

My intention for the day:

....

....

....

A belief / habit to change:

....

....

....

What I can do today to get me closer to where I want to be tomorrow:

....

....

....

My daily affirmation:

....

....

....

EVENING REFLECTION

Date:..................

How I Feel Before Sleep

Hmmm.... Peaceful / Grateful

0 1 2 3 4 5 6 7 8 9 10

What did I learn today?

....

....

....

How I showed or received kindness today (others/self):

....

....

....

How I connected with nature today:

....

....

....

Something I did or said which took courage:

....

....

....

Who (which part of me) will show up tomorrow to make the day even better?

Creator / Magician ☐ ....

Warrior / Courage ☐ ....

Leader / Inspiration ☐ ....

Love / Authentic Self ☐

Is What I Am Doing Today Getting Me Closer To Where I Want To Be Tomorrow

?

MORNING REFLECTION

My Power Word: "   "Date:..................

Hmmm....   How I Feel Right Now   Great

0 1 2 3 4 5 6 7 8 9 10

Today I'm grateful for:

....

....

....

My intention for the day:

....

....

....

A belief / habit to change:

....

....

....

What I can do today to get me closer to where I want to be tomorrow:

....

....

....

My daily affirmation:

....

....

....

EVENING REFLECTION

Date:..................

How I Feel Before Sleep

Hmmm.... Peaceful / Grateful

0 1 2 3 4 5 6 7 8 9 10

What did I learn today?

....

....

....

How I showed or received kindness today (others/self):

....

....

....

How I connected with nature today:

....

....

....

Something I did or said which took courage:

....

....

....

Who (which part of me) will show up tomorrow to make the day even better?

- Creator / Magician ☐
- Warrior / Courage ☐
- Leader / Inspiration ☐
- Love / Authentic Self ☐

....

....

....

MORNING REFLECTION

My Power Word: "   "Date:.................

Hmmm....   How I Feel Right Now   Great

0 1 2 3 4 5 6 7 8 9 10

Today I'm grateful for:

....

....

....

My intention for the day:

....

....

....

A belief / habit to change:

....

....

....

What I can do today to get me closer to where I want to be tomorrow:

....

....

....

My daily affirmation:

....

....

....

EVENING REFLECTION

Date:..................

How I Feel Before Sleep

Hmmm.... Peaceful / Grateful

0 1 2 3 4 5 6 7 8 9 10

What did I learn today?

How I showed or received kindness today (others/self):

How I connected with nature today:

Something I did or said which took courage:

Who (which part of me) will show up tomorrow to make the day even better?

Creator / Magician ☐

Warrior / Courage ☐

Leader / Inspiration ☐

Love / Authentic Self ☐

bonus day

My Power Word:

Date:

Mood/Emotion Tracker

○ ○ ○ ○ ○

SAD / LOW ⟷ HAPPY / ENERGISED

I am Grateful for:

My Intention / Focus for today:

Space for Creativity

DOODLE, COLOUR, WORDS, THOUGHTS

My Purpose / Mission:

What I GET to do today:

MORNING REFLECTION

My Power Word: "   "Date:..................

Hmmm....   How I Feel Right Now   Great

0 1 2 3 4 5 6 7 8 9 10

Today I'm grateful for:

...

...

...

My intention for the day:

...

...

...

A belief / habit to change:

...

...

...

What I can do today to get me closer to where I want to be tomorrow:

...

...

...

My daily affirmation:

...

...

...

EVENING REFLECTION

Date:..................

How I Feel Before Sleep

Hmmm.... Peaceful / Grateful

0 1 2 3 4 5 6 7 8 9 10

What did I learn today?

How I showed or received kindness today (others/self):

How I connected with nature today:

Something I did or said which took courage:

Who (which part of me) will show up tomorrow to make the day even better?

Creator / Magician

Warrior / Courage

Leader / Inspiration

Love / Authentic Self

MORNING REFLECTION

My Power Word: " " Date:.................

Hmmm.... How I Feel Right Now Great

0 1 2 3 4 5 6 7 8 9 10

Today I'm grateful for:

My intention for the day:

A belief / habit to change:

What I can do today to get me closer to where I want to be tomorrow:

My daily affirmation:

EVENING REFLECTION

Date:..................

How I Feel Before Sleep

Hmmm.... Peaceful / Grateful

0 1 2 3 4 5 6 7 8 9 10

What did I learn today?

How I showed or received kindness today (others/self):

How I connected with nature today:

Something I did or said which took courage:

Who (which part of me) will show up tomorrow to make the day even better?

Creator / Magician

Warrior / Courage

Leader / Inspiration

Love / Authentic Self

MORNING REFLECTION

My Power Word: "   "Date:..................

Hmmm....   How I Feel Right Now   Great

0 1 2 3 4 5 6 7 8 9 10

Today I'm grateful for:

....

....

....

My intention for the day:

....

....

....

A belief / habit to change:

....

....

....

What I can do today to get me closer to where I want to be tomorrow:

....

....

....

My daily affirmation:

....

....

....

EVENING REFLECTION

Date:..................

How I Feel Before Sleep

Hmmm.... Peaceful / Grateful

0 1 2 3 4 5 6 7 8 9 10

What did I learn today?

How I showed or received kindness today (others/self):

How I connected with nature today:

Something I did or said which took courage:

Who (which part of me) will show up tomorrow to make the day even better?

Creator / Magician

Warrior / Courage

Leader / Inspiration

Love / Authentic Self

MORNING REFLECTION

My Power Word: "   " Date:..................

Hmmm....   How I Feel Right Now   Great

0 1 2 3 4 5 6 7 8 9 10

Today I'm grateful for:

....

....

....

My intention for the day:

....

....

....

A belief / habit to change:

....

....

....

What I can do today to get me closer to where I want to be tomorrow:

....

....

....

My daily affirmation:

....

....

....

EVENING REFLECTION

Date:..................

How I Feel Before Sleep

Hmmm.... Peaceful / Grateful

0 1 2 3 4 5 6 7 8 9 10

What did I learn today?

....

....

....

How I showed or received kindness today (others/self):

....

....

....

How I connected with nature today:

....

....

....

Something I did or said which took courage:

....

....

....

Who (which part of me) will show up tomorrow to make the day even better?

- Creator / Magician ☐
- Warrior / Courage ☐
- Leader / Inspiration ☐
- Love / Authentic Self ☐

....

....

....

MORNING REFLECTION

My Power Word: "   " Date:.................

Hmmm....   How I Feel Right Now   Great

0 1 2 3 4 5 6 7 8 9 10

Today I'm grateful for:

My intention for the day:

A belief / habit to change:

What I can do today to get me closer to where I want to be tomorrow:

My daily affirmation:

EVENING REFLECTION

Date:..................

How I Feel Before Sleep

Hmmm.... Peaceful / Grateful

0 1 2 3 4 5 6 7 8 9 10

What did I learn today?

How I showed or received kindness today (others/self):

How I connected with nature today:

Something I did or said which took courage:

Who (which part of me) will show up tomorrow to make the day even better?

Creator / Magician ☐

Warrior / Courage ☐

Leader / Inspiration ☐

Love / Authentic Self ☐

Have The Courage To Really Live Life With Purpose, Passion And Energy...And You'll Notice What Happens

MORNING REFLECTION

My Power Word: "   "Date:..................

Hmmm....   How I Feel Right Now   Great

0 1 2 3 4 5 6 7 8 9 10

Today I'm grateful for:

....

....

....

My intention for the day:

....

....

....

A belief / habit to change:

....

....

....

What I can do today to get me closer to where I want to be tomorrow:

....

....

....

My daily affirmation:

....

....

....

EVENING REFLECTION

Date:..................

How I Feel Before Sleep

Hmmm.... Peaceful / Grateful

0 1 2 3 4 5 6 7 8 9 10

What did I learn today?

....

....

....

How I showed or received kindness today (others/self):

....

....

....

How I connected with nature today:

....

....

....

Something I did or said which took courage:

....

....

....

Who (which part of me) will show up tomorrow to make the day even better?

- Creator / Magician ☐
- Warrior / Courage ☐
- Leader / Inspiration ☐
- Love / Authentic Self ☐

....

....

....

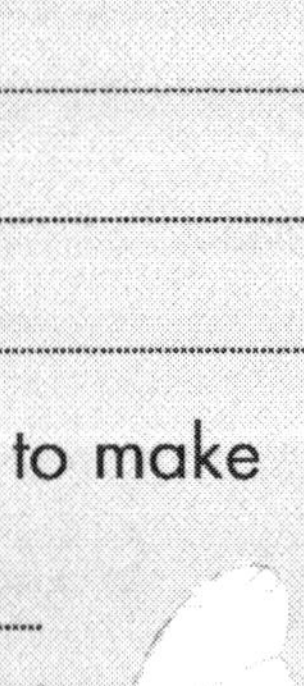

MORNING REFLECTION

My Power Word: " **"Date:..................**

Hmmm.... **How I Feel Right Now** Great

0 1 2 3 4 5 6 7 8 9 10

Today I'm grateful for:

My intention for the day:

A belief / habit to change:

What I can do today to get me closer to where I want to be tomorrow:

My daily affirmation:

EVENING REFLECTION

Date:..................

How I Feel Before Sleep

Hmmm.... Peaceful / Grateful

0 1 2 3 4 5 6 7 8 9 10

What did I learn today?

How I showed or received kindness today (others/self):

How I connected with nature today:

Something I did or said which took courage:

Who (which part of me) will show up tomorrow to make the day even better?

- Creator / Magician ☐
- Warrior / Courage ☐
- Leader / Inspiration ☐
- Love / Authentic Self ☐

MORNING REFLECTION

My Power Word: " "Date:..................

Hmmm.... **How I Feel Right Now** Great

0 1 2 3 4 5 6 7 8 9 10

Today I'm grateful for:

My intention for the day:

A belief / habit to change:

What I can do today to get me closer to where I want to be tomorrow:

My daily affirmation:

EVENING REFLECTION

Date:..................

How I Feel Before Sleep

Hmmm.... Peaceful / Grateful

0 1 2 3 4 5 6 7 8 9 10

What did I learn today?

....

....

....

How I showed or received kindness today (others/self):

....

....

....

How I connected with nature today:

....

....

....

Something I did or said which took courage:

....

....

....

Who (which part of me) will show up tomorrow to make the day even better?

- Creator / Magician ☐
- Warrior / Courage ☐
- Leader / Inspiration ☐
- Love / Authentic Self ☐

....

....

....

MORNING REFLECTION

My Power Word: "   "Date:..................

Hmmm....   How I Feel Right Now   Great

0 1 2 3 4 5 6 7 8 9 10

Today I'm grateful for:

....

....

....

My intention for the day:

....

....

....

A belief / habit to change:

....

....

....

What I can do today to get me closer to where I want to be tomorrow:

....

....

....

My daily affirmation:

....

....

....

EVENING REFLECTION

Date:..................

How I Feel Before Sleep

Hmmm.... Peaceful / Grateful

0 1 2 3 4 5 6 7 8 9 10

What did I learn today?

....

....

....

How I showed or received kindness today (others/self):

....

....

....

How I connected with nature today:

....

....

....

Something I did or said which took courage:

....

....

....

Who (which part of me) will show up tomorrow to make the day even better?

- Creator / Magician ☐
- Warrior / Courage ☐
- Leader / Inspiration ☐
- Love / Authentic Self ☐

....

....

....

MORNING REFLECTION

My Power Word: "   "Date:..................

Hmmm.... How I Feel Right Now Great

0 1 2 3 4 5 6 7 8 9 10

Today I'm grateful for:

....

....

....

My intention for the day:

....

....

....

A belief / habit to change:

....

....

....

What I can do today to get me closer to where I want to be tomorrow:

....

....

....

My daily affirmation:

....

....

....

EVENING REFLECTION

Date:..................

How I Feel Before Sleep

Hmmm.... Peaceful / Grateful

0 1 2 3 4 5 6 7 8 9 10

What did I learn today?

How I showed or received kindness today (others/self):

How I connected with nature today:

Something I did or said which took courage:

Who (which part of me) will show up tomorrow to make the day even better?

Creator / Magician

Warrior / Courage

Leader / Inspiration

Love / Authentic Self

MORNING REFLECTION

My Power Word: "   "Date:.................

Hmmm....   How I Feel Right Now   Great

0 1 2 3 4 5 6 7 8 9 10

Today I'm grateful for:

....

....

....

My intention for the day:

....

....

....

A belief / habit to change:

....

....

....

What I can do today to get me closer to where I want to be tomorrow:

....

....

....

My daily affirmation:

....

....

....

EVENING REFLECTION

Date:..................

How I Feel Before Sleep

Hmmm... Peaceful / Grateful

0 1 2 3 4 5 6 7 8 9 10

What did I learn today?

....

....

....

How I showed or received kindness today (others/self):

....

....

....

How I connected with nature today:

....

....

....

Something I did or said which took courage:

....

....

....

Who (which part of me) will show up tomorrow to make the day even better?

- Creator / Magician ☐
- Warrior / Courage ☐
- Leader / Inspiration ☐
- Love / Authentic Self ☐

....

....

....

MORNING REFLECTION

My Power Word: "   " Date:.................

Hmmm.... How I Feel Right Now Great

0 1 2 3 4 5 6 7 8 9 10

Today I'm grateful for:

....

....

....

My intention for the day:

....

....

....

A belief / habit to change:

....

....

....

What I can do today to get me closer to where I want to be tomorrow:

....

....

....

My daily affirmation:

....

....

....

EVENING REFLECTION

Date:..................

How I Feel Before Sleep

Hmmm.... Peaceful / Grateful

0 1 2 3 4 5 6 7 8 9 10

What did I learn today?

....

....

....

How I showed or received kindness today (others/self):

....

....

....

How I connected with nature today:

....

....

....

Something I did or said which took courage:

....

....

....

Who (which part of me) will show up tomorrow to make the day even better?

- [ ] Creator / Magician
- [ ] Warrior / Courage
- [ ] Leader / Inspiration
- [ ] Love / Authentic Self

____

____

____

MORNING REFLECTION

My Power Word: " "Date:.................

Hmmm.... How I Feel Right Now Great

0 1 2 3 4 5 6 7 8 9 10

Today I'm grateful for:

....

....

....

My intention for the day:

....

....

....

A belief / habit to change:

....

....

....

What I can do today to get me closer to where I want to be tomorrow:

....

....

....

My daily affirmation:

....

....

....

EVENING REFLECTION

Date:..................

How I Feel Before Sleep

Hmmm.... Peaceful / Grateful

0 1 2 3 4 5 6 7 8 9 10

What did I learn today?

How I showed or received kindness today (others/self):

How I connected with nature today:

Something I did or said which took courage:

Who (which part of me) will show up tomorrow to make the day even better?

- Creator / Magician ☐
- Warrior / Courage ☐
- Leader / Inspiration ☐
- Love / Authentic Self ☐

MORNING REFLECTION

My Power Word: "   "Date:..................

Hmmm....   How I Feel Right Now   Great

0 1 2 3 4 5 6 7 8 9 10

Today I'm grateful for:

....

....

....

My intention for the day:

....

....

....

A belief / habit to change:

....

....

....

What I can do today to get me closer to where I want to be tomorrow:

....

....

....

My daily affirmation:

....

....

....

EVENING REFLECTION

Date:..................

How I Feel Before Sleep

Hmmm... Peaceful / Grateful

0 1 2 3 4 5 6 7 8 9 10

What did I learn today?

How I showed or received kindness today (others/self):

How I connected with nature today:

Something I did or said which took courage:

Who (which part of me) will show up tomorrow to make the day even better?

- Creator / Magician ☐
- Warrior / Courage ☐
- Leader / Inspiration ☐
- Love / Authentic Self ☐

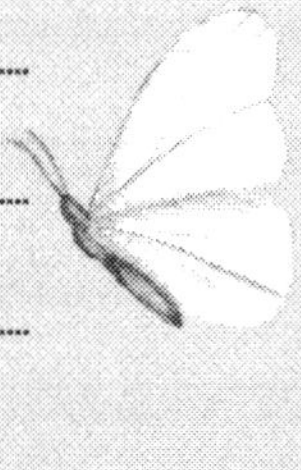

MORNING REFLECTION

My Power Word: " "Date:..................

Hmmm.... **How I Feel Right Now** Great

0 1 2 3 4 5 6 7 8 9 10

Today I'm grateful for:

My intention for the day:

A belief / habit to change:

What I can do today to get me closer to where I want to be tomorrow:

My daily affirmation:

EVENING REFLECTION

Date:..................

How I Feel Before Sleep

Hmmm.... Peaceful / Grateful

0 1 2 3 4 5 6 7 8 9 10

What did I learn today?

....

....

....

How I showed or received kindness today (others/self):

....

....

....

How I connected with nature today:

....

....

....

Something I did or said which took courage:

....

....

....

Who (which part of me) will show up tomorrow to make the day even better?

- Creator / Magician ☐ ....
- Warrior / Courage ☐ ....
- Leader / Inspiration ☐ ....
- Love / Authentic Self ☐

MORNING REFLECTION

My Power Word: "   "Date:..................

Hmmm.... How I Feel Right Now Great

0 1 2 3 4 5 6 7 8 9 10

Today I'm grateful for:

....

....

....

My intention for the day:

....

....

....

A belief / habit to change:

....

....

....

What I can do today to get me closer to where I want to be tomorrow:

....

....

....

My daily affirmation:

....

....

....

EVENING REFLECTION

Date:..................

How I Feel Before Sleep

Hmmm.... Peaceful / Grateful

0 1 2 3 4 5 6 7 8 9 10

What did I learn today?

....

....

....

How I showed or received kindness today (others/self):

....

....

....

How I connected with nature today:

....

....

....

Something I did or said which took courage:

....

....

....

Who (which part of me) will show up tomorrow to make the day even better?

- Creator / Magician ☐
- Warrior / Courage ☐
- Leader / Inspiration ☐
- Love / Authentic Self ☐

....

....

....

Nature is My Recluse

Nature is my recluse, Nature is my home,
Nature is the one who speaks to my soul.

Nature invites me, it makes me feel whole,
Nature supports me and welcomes all my woes.

Nature invites me to take things slow,
Nature reminds me it's okay not to know.

Nature protects & strengthens all souls,
Nature is the one that cannot be controlled.

Nature is magical, it transforms & renews,
Nature is all powerful, it will never subdue.

Nature is hopeful with its sweet, pure song.
And I am thankful that in Nature
Is right where I belong.

Poem by
Deirdre Whitmore

© copyright Deirdre Whitmore 2024

MORNING REFLECTION

My Power Word: " "Date:.................

Hmmm.... How I Feel Right Now Great

0 1 2 3 4 5 6 7 8 9 10

Today I'm grateful for:

....

....

....

My intention for the day:

....

....

....

A belief / habit to change:

....

....

....

What I can do today to get me closer to where I want to be tomorrow:

....

....

....

My daily affirmation:

....

....

....

EVENING REFLECTION

Date:..................

How I Feel Before Sleep

Hmmm.... Peaceful / Grateful

0 1 2 3 4 5 6 7 8 9 10

What did I learn today?

....

....

....

How I showed or received kindness today (others/self):

....

....

....

How I connected with nature today:

....

....

....

Something I did or said which took courage:

....

....

....

Who (which part of me) will show up tomorrow to make the day even better?

- Creator / Magician ☐
- Warrior / Courage ☐
- Leader / Inspiration ☐
- Love / Authentic Self ☐

....

....

....

MORNING REFLECTION

My Power Word: " "Date:..................

Hmmm.... How I Feel Right Now Great

0 1 2 3 4 5 6 7 8 9 10

Today I'm grateful for:

My intention for the day:

A belief / habit to change:

What I can do today to get me closer to where I want to be tomorrow:

My daily affirmation:

EVENING REFLECTION

Date:..................

How I Feel Before Sleep

Hmmm... Peaceful / Grateful

0 1 2 3 4 5 6 7 8 9 10

What did I learn today?

....

....

....

How I showed or received kindness today (others/self):

....

....

....

How I connected with nature today:

....

....

....

Something I did or said which took courage:

....

....

....

Who (which part of me) will show up tomorrow to make the day even better?

- Creator / Magician ☐
- Warrior / Courage ☐
- Leader / Inspiration ☐
- Love / Authentic Self ☐

....

....

....

MORNING REFLECTION

My Power Word: " " Date:..................

Hmmm.... How I Feel Right Now Great

0 1 2 3 4 5 6 7 8 9 10

Today I'm grateful for:

....

....

....

My intention for the day:

....

....

....

A belief / habit to change:

....

....

....

What I can do today to get me closer to where I want to be tomorrow:

....

....

....

My daily affirmation:

....

....

....

EVENING REFLECTION

Date:..................

How I Feel Before Sleep

Hmmm.... Peaceful / Grateful

0 1 2 3 4 5 6 7 8 9 10

What did I learn today?

....

....

....

How I showed or received kindness today (others/self):

....

....

....

How I connected with nature today:

....

....

....

Something I did or said which took courage:

....

....

....

Who (which part of me) will show up tomorrow to make the day even better?

- Creator / Magician ☐
- Warrior / Courage ☐
- Leader / Inspiration ☐
- Love / Authentic Self ☐

....

....

....

bonus day

My Power Word:

Date:

Mood/Emotion Tracker

○ ○ ○ ○ ○

SAD / LOW ⟷ HAPPY / ENERGISED

Space for Creativity

DOODLE, COLOUR, WORDS, THOUGHTS

I am Grateful for:

My Intention / Focus for today:

My Purpose / Mission:

What I GET to do today:

MORNING REFLECTION

My Power Word: "   "Date:.................

Hmmm....   How I Feel Right Now   Great

0   1   2   3   4   5   6   7   8   9   10

Today I'm grateful for:

....

....

....

My intention for the day:

....

....

....

A belief / habit to change:

....

....

....

What I can do today to get me closer to where I want to be tomorrow:

....

....

....

My daily affirmation:

....

....

....

EVENING REFLECTION

Date:..................

How I Feel Before Sleep

Hmmm.... Peaceful / Grateful

0 1 2 3 4 5 6 7 8 9 10

What did I learn today?

....

....

....

How I showed or received kindness today (others/self):

....

....

....

How I connected with nature today:

....

....

....

Something I did or said which took courage:

....

....

....

Who (which part of me) will show up tomorrow to make the day even better?

- Creator / Magician ☐
- Warrior / Courage ☐
- Leader / Inspiration ☐
- Love / Authentic Self ☐

....

....

....

MORNING REFLECTION

My Power Word: "   "Date:..................

Hmmm....   How I Feel Right Now   Great

0 1 2 3 4 5 6 7 8 9 10

Today I'm grateful for:

....

....

....

My intention for the day:

....

....

....

A belief / habit to change:

....

....

....

What I can do today to get me closer to where I want to be tomorrow:

....

....

....

My daily affirmation:

....

....

....

EVENING REFLECTION

Date:..................

How I Feel Before Sleep

Hmmm.... Peaceful / Grateful

0 1 2 3 4 5 6 7 8 9 10

What did I learn today?

....

....

....

How I showed or received kindness today (others/self):

....

....

....

How I connected with nature today:

....

....

....

Something I did or said which took courage:

....

....

....

Who (which part of me) will show up tomorrow to make the day even better?

Creator / Magician ☐

Warrior / Courage ☐

Leader / Inspiration ☐

Love / Authentic Self ☐

MORNING REFLECTION

My Power Word: " "Date:.................

Hmmm.... How I Feel Right Now Great

0 1 2 3 4 5 6 7 8 9 10

Today I'm grateful for:

My intention for the day:

A belief / habit to change:

What I can do today to get me closer to where I want to be tomorrow:

My daily affirmation:

EVENING REFLECTION

Date:..................

How I Feel Before Sleep

Hmmm.... Peaceful / Grateful

0 1 2 3 4 5 6 7 8 9 10

What did I learn today?

....

....

....

How I showed or received kindness today (others/self):

....

....

....

How I connected with nature today:

....

....

....

Something I did or said which took courage:

....

....

....

Who (which part of me) will show up tomorrow to make the day even better?

- Creator / Magician ☐
- Warrior / Courage ☐
- Leader / Inspiration ☐
- Love / Authentic Self ☐

....

....

....

MORNING REFLECTION

My Power Word: "   " Date:..................

Hmmm....   How I Feel Right Now   Great

0 1 2 3 4 5 6 7 8 9 10

Today I'm grateful for:

....

....

....

My intention for the day:

....

....

....

A belief / habit to change:

....

....

....

What I can do today to get me closer to where I want to be tomorrow:

....

....

....

My daily affirmation:

....

....

....

EVENING REFLECTION

Date:..................

How I Feel Before Sleep

Hmmm.... Peaceful / Grateful

0 1 2 3 4 5 6 7 8 9 10

What did I learn today?

....

....

....

How I showed or received kindness today (others/self):

....

....

....

How I connected with nature today:

....

....

....

Something I did or said which took courage:

....

....

....

Who (which part of me) will show up tomorrow to make the day even better?

Creator / Magician ☐ ....

Warrior / Courage ☐ ....

Leader / Inspiration ☐ ....

Love / Authentic Self ☐

MORNING REFLECTION

My Power Word: "............ Date:.................

Hmmm.... **How I Feel Right Now** Great

0 1 2 3 4 5 6 7 8 9 10

Today I'm grateful for:

....

....

....

My intention for the day:

....

....

....

A belief / habit to change:

....

....

....

What I can do today to get me closer to where I want to be tomorrow:

....

....

....

My daily affirmation:

....

....

....

EVENING REFLECTION

Date:..................

How I Feel Before Sleep

Hmmm... Peaceful / Grateful

0 1 2 3 4 5 6 7 8 9 10

What did I learn today?

....

....

....

How I showed or received kindness today (others/self):

....

....

....

How I connected with nature today:

....

....

....

Something I did or said which took courage:

....

....

....

Who (which part of me) will show up tomorrow to make the day even better?

- Creator / Magician ☐
- Warrior / Courage ☐
- Leader / Inspiration ☐
- Love / Authentic Self ☐

....

....

....

MORNING REFLECTION

My Power Word: ” “Date:..................

Hmmm.... **How I Feel Right Now** Great

0 1 2 3 4 5 6 7 8 9 10

Today I'm grateful for:

....

....

....

My intention for the day:

....

....

....

A belief / habit to change:

....

....

....

What I can do today to get me closer to where I want to be tomorrow:

....

....

....

My daily affirmation:

....

....

....

EVENING REFLECTION

Date:..................

How I Feel Before Sleep

Hmmm.... Peaceful / Grateful

0 1 2 3 4 5 6 7 8 9 10

What did I learn today?

How I showed or received kindness today (others/self):

How I connected with nature today:

Something I did or said which took courage:

Who (which part of me) will show up tomorrow to make the day even better?

- Creator / Magician
- Warrior / Courage
- Leader / Inspiration
- Love / Authentic Self

MORNING REFLECTION

My Power Word: ”   “Date:.................

Hmmm....   How I Feel Right Now   Great

0 1 2 3 4 5 6 7 8 9 10

Today I'm grateful for:

My intention for the day:

A belief / habit to change:

What I can do today to get me closer to where I want to be tomorrow:

My daily affirmation:

EVENING REFLECTION

Date:..................

How I Feel Before Sleep

Hmmm.... Peaceful / Grateful

0 1 2 3 4 5 6 7 8 9 10

What did I learn today?

How I showed or received kindness today (others/self):

How I connected with nature today:

Something I did or said which took courage:

Who (which part of me) will show up tomorrow to make the day even better?

Creator / Magician ☐

Warrior / Courage ☐

Leader / Inspiration ☐

Love / Authentic Self ☐

MORNING REFLECTION

My Power Word: "   " Date:..................

Hmmm....   How I Feel Right Now   Great

0 1 2 3 4 5 6 7 8 9 10

Today I'm grateful for:

....

....

....

My intention for the day:

....

....

....

A belief / habit to change:

....

....

....

What I can do today to get me closer to where I want to be tomorrow:

....

....

....

My daily affirmation:

....

....

....

EVENING REFLECTION

Date:..................

How I Feel Before Sleep

Hmmm.... Peaceful / Grateful

0 1 2 3 4 5 6 7 8 9 10

What did I learn today?

....

....

....

How I showed or received kindness today (others/self):

....

....

....

How I connected with nature today:

....

....

....

Something I did or said which took courage:

....

....

....

Who (which part of me) will show up tomorrow to make the day even better?

- Creator / Magician ☐
- Warrior / Courage ☐
- Leader / Inspiration ☐
- Love / Authentic Self ☐

....

....

....

bonus day

My Power Word:

Date:

Mood/Emotion Tracker

○ ○ ○ ○ ○

SAD / LOW ⟷ HAPPY / ENERGISED

Space for Creativity

DOODLE, COLOUR, WORDS, THOUGHTS

I am Grateful for:

My Intention / Focus for today:

My Purpose / Mission:

What I GET to do today:

MORNING REFLECTION

My Power Word: "   " Date:.................

Hmmm.... **How I Feel Right Now** Great

0 1 2 3 4 5 6 7 8 9 10

Today I'm grateful for:

....

....

....

My intention for the day:

....

....

....

A belief / habit to change:

....

....

....

What I can do today to get me closer to where I want to be tomorrow:

....

....

....

My daily affirmation:

....

....

....

EVENING REFLECTION

Date:..................

How I Feel Before Sleep

Hmmm.... Peaceful / Grateful

0 1 2 3 4 5 6 7 8 9 10

What did I learn today?

....

....

....

How I showed or received kindness today (others/self):

....

....

....

How I connected with nature today:

....

....

....

Something I did or said which took courage:

....

....

....

Who (which part of me) will show up tomorrow to make the day even better?

- Creator / Magician ☐
- Warrior / Courage ☐
- Leader / Inspiration ☐
- Love / Authentic Self ☐

....

....

....

MORNING REFLECTION

My Power Word: "   "Date:.................

Hmmm....   How I Feel Right Now   Great

0 1 2 3 4 5 6 7 8 9 10

Today I'm grateful for:

....

....

....

My intention for the day:

....

....

....

A belief / habit to change:

....

....

....

What I can do today to get me closer to where I want to be tomorrow:

....

....

....

My daily affirmation:

....

....

....

EVENING REFLECTION

Date:..................

How I Feel Before Sleep

Hmmm... Peaceful / Grateful

0 1 2 3 4 5 6 7 8 9 10

What did I learn today?

....

....

....

How I showed or received kindness today (others/self):

....

....

....

How I connected with nature today:

....

....

....

Something I did or said which took courage:

....

....

....

Who (which part of me) will show up tomorrow to make the day even better?

- Creator / Magician ☐
- Warrior / Courage ☐
- Leader / Inspiration ☐
- Love / Authentic Self ☐

....

....

....

MORNING REFLECTION

My Power Word: " " Date:.................

Hmmm.... How I Feel Right Now Great

0 1 2 3 4 5 6 7 8 9 10

Today I'm grateful for:

....

....

....

My intention for the day:

....

....

....

A belief / habit to change:

....

....

....

What I can do today to get me closer to where I want to be tomorrow:

....

....

....

My daily affirmation:

....

....

....

EVENING REFLECTION

Date:..................

How I Feel Before Sleep

Hmmm.... Peaceful / Grateful

0 1 2 3 4 5 6 7 8 9 10

What did I learn today?

How I showed or received kindness today (others/self):

How I connected with nature today:

Something I did or said which took courage:

Who (which part of me) will show up tomorrow to make the day even better?

- Creator / Magician ☐
- Warrior / Courage ☐
- Leader / Inspiration ☐
- Love / Authentic Self ☐

bonus day

My Power Word:

Date:

Mood/Emotion Tracker

○ ○ ○ ○ ○

SAD / LOW ⟷ HAPPY / ENERGISED

I am Grateful for:

My Intention / Focus for today:

Space for Creativity

DOODLE, COLOUR, WORDS, THOUGHTS

My Purpose / Mission:

What I GET to do today:

MORNING REFLECTION

My Power Word: ” **“Date:.................**

Hmmm.... **How I Feel Right Now** Great

0 1 2 3 4 5 6 7 8 9 10

Today I'm grateful for:

My intention for the day:

A belief / habit to change:

What I can do today to get me closer to where I want to be tomorrow:

My daily affirmation:

EVENING REFLECTION

Date:..................

How I Feel Before Sleep

Hmmm.... 0 1 2 3 4 5 6 7 8 9 10 Peaceful / Grateful

What did I learn today?

How I showed or received kindness today (others/self):

How I connected with nature today:

Something I did or said which took courage:

Who (which part of me) will show up tomorrow to make the day even better?

Creator / Magician ☐

Warrior / Courage ☐

Leader / Inspiration ☐

Love / Authentic Self ☐

MORNING REFLECTION

My Power Word: "   "Date:..................

Hmmm....   How I Feel Right Now   Great

0 1 2 3 4 5 6 7 8 9 10

Today I'm grateful for:

....

....

....

My intention for the day:

....

....

....

A belief / habit to change:

....

....

....

What I can do today to get me closer to where I want to be tomorrow:

....

....

....

My daily affirmation:

....

....

....

EVENING REFLECTION

Date:..................

How I Feel Before Sleep

Hmmm.... Peaceful / Grateful

0 1 2 3 4 5 6 7 8 9 10

What did I learn today?

How I showed or received kindness today (others/self):

How I connected with nature today:

Something I did or said which took courage:

Who (which part of me) will show up tomorrow to make the day even better?

Creator / Magician

Warrior / Courage

Leader / Inspiration

Love / Authentic Self

MORNING REFLECTION

My Power Word: "   "Date:..................

Hmmm....   How I Feel Right Now   Great

0 1 2 3 4 5 6 7 8 9 10

Today I'm grateful for:

....

....

....

My intention for the day:

....

....

....

A belief / habit to change:

....

....

....

What I can do today to get me closer to where I want to be tomorrow:

....

....

....

My daily affirmation:

....

....

....

EVENING REFLECTION

Date:..................

How I Feel Before Sleep

Hmmm.... Peaceful / Grateful

0 1 2 3 4 5 6 7 8 9 10

What did I learn today?

....

....

....

How I showed or received kindness today (others/self):

....

....

....

How I connected with nature today:

....

....

....

Something I did or said which took courage:

....

....

....

Who (which part of me) will show up tomorrow to make the day even better?

- Creator / Magician ☐
- Warrior / Courage ☐
- Leader / Inspiration ☐
- Love / Authentic Self ☐

....

....

....

MORNING REFLECTION

My Power Word: "   "Date:.................

Hmmm....   How I Feel Right Now   Great

0   1   2   3   4   5   6   7   8   9   10

Today I'm grateful for:

....

....

....

My intention for the day:

....

....

....

A belief / habit to change:

....

....

....

What I can do today to get me closer to where I want to be tomorrow:

....

....

....

My daily affirmation:

....

....

....

EVENING REFLECTION

Date:..................

How I Feel Before Sleep

Hmmm.... Peaceful / Grateful

0 1 2 3 4 5 6 7 8 9 10

What did I learn today?

How I showed or received kindness today (others/self):

How I connected with nature today:

Something I did or said which took courage:

Who (which part of me) will show up tomorrow to make the day even better?

- Creator / Magician ☐
- Warrior / Courage ☐
- Leader / Inspiration ☐
- Love / Authentic Self ☐

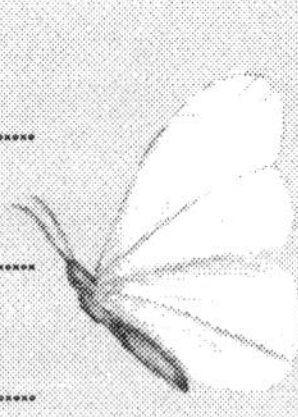

MORNING REFLECTION

My Power Word: "   "Date:.................

Hmmm....   How I Feel Right Now   Great

0 1 2 3 4 5 6 7 8 9 10

Today I'm grateful for:

....

....

....

My intention for the day:

....

....

....

A belief / habit to change:

....

....

....

What I can do today to get me closer to where I want to be tomorrow:

....

....

....

My daily affirmation:

....

....

....

EVENING REFLECTION

Date:..................

How I Feel Before Sleep

Hmmm... Peaceful / Grateful

0 1 2 3 4 5 6 7 8 9 10

What did I learn today?

....

....

....

How I showed or received kindness today (others/self):

....

....

....

How I connected with nature today:

....

....

....

Something I did or said which took courage:

....

....

....

Who (which part of me) will show up tomorrow to make the day even better?

- Creator / Magician ☐ ....
- Warrior / Courage ☐ ....
- Leader / Inspiration ☐ ....
- Love / Authentic Self ☐

MORNING REFLECTION

My Power Word: " "Date:.................

Hmmm.... **How I Feel Right Now** Great

0 1 2 3 4 5 6 7 8 9 10

Today I'm grateful for:

....

....

....

My intention for the day:

....

....

....

A belief / habit to change:

....

....

....

What I can do today to get me closer to where I want to be tomorrow:

....

....

....

My daily affirmation:

....

....

....

EVENING REFLECTION

Date:..................

How I Feel Before Sleep

Hmmm.... 0 1 2 3 4 5 6 7 8 9 10 Peaceful / Grateful

What did I learn today?

How I showed or received kindness today (others/self):

How I connected with nature today:

Something I did or said which took courage:

Who (which part of me) will show up tomorrow to make the day even better?

Creator / Magician ☐

Warrior / Courage ☐

Leader / Inspiration ☐

Love / Authentic Self ☐

MORNING REFLECTION

My Power Word: "   "Date:..................

Hmmm.... **How I Feel Right Now** Great

0 1 2 3 4 5 6 7 8 9 10

Today I'm grateful for:

My intention for the day:

A belief / habit to change:

What I can do today to get me closer to where I want to be tomorrow:

My daily affirmation:

EVENING REFLECTION

Date:..................

How I Feel Before Sleep

Hmmm.... Peaceful / Grateful

0 1 2 3 4 5 6 7 8 9 10

What did I learn today?

How I showed or received kindness today (others/self):

How I connected with nature today:

Something I did or said which took courage:

Who (which part of me) will show up tomorrow to make the day even better?

- Creator / Magician ☐
- Warrior / Courage ☐
- Leader / Inspiration ☐
- Love / Authentic Self ☐

Acceptance...
Accepting the things we *can't* change and the things we *can* change = peace

MORNING REFLECTION

My Power Word: " "Date:..................

Hmmm.... How I Feel Right Now Great

0 1 2 3 4 5 6 7 8 9 10

Today I'm grateful for:

....

....

....

My intention for the day:

....

....

....

A belief / habit to change:

....

....

....

What I can do today to get me closer to where I want to be tomorrow:

....

....

....

My daily affirmation:

....

....

....

EVENING REFLECTION

Date:..................

How I Feel Before Sleep

Hmmm.... Peaceful / Grateful

0 1 2 3 4 5 6 7 8 9 10

What did I learn today?

How I showed or received kindness today (others/self):

How I connected with nature today:

Something I did or said which took courage:

Who (which part of me) will show up tomorrow to make the day even better?

- Creator / Magician ☐
- Warrior / Courage ☐
- Leader / Inspiration ☐
- Love / Authentic Self ☐

MORNING REFLECTION

My Power Word: "   " Date:.................

Hmmm.... **How I Feel Right Now** Great

0 1 2 3 4 5 6 7 8 9 10

Today I'm grateful for:

....

....

....

My intention for the day:

....

....

....

A belief / habit to change:

....

....

....

What I can do today to get me closer to where I want to be tomorrow:

....

....

....

My daily affirmation:

....

....

....

EVENING REFLECTION

Date:..................

How I Feel Before Sleep

Hmmm.... Peaceful / Grateful

0 1 2 3 4 5 6 7 8 9 10

What did I learn today?

How I showed or received kindness today (others/self):

How I connected with nature today:

Something I did or said which took courage:

Who (which part of me) will show up tomorrow to make the day even better?

Creator / Magician

Warrior / Courage

Leader / Inspiration

Love / Authentic Self

MORNING REFLECTION

My Power Word: "　　　　　　　　　　" Date:.................

Hmmm.... **How I Feel Right Now** Great

0 1 2 3 4 5 6 7 8 9 10

Today I'm grateful for:

....

....

....

My intention for the day:

....

....

....

A belief / habit to change:

....

....

....

What I can do today to get me closer to where I want to be tomorrow:

....

....

....

My daily affirmation:

....

....

....

EVENING REFLECTION

Date:..................

How I Feel Before Sleep

Hmmm.... Peaceful / Grateful

0 1 2 3 4 5 6 7 8 9 10

What did I learn today?

....

....

....

How I showed or received kindness today (others/self):

....

....

....

How I connected with nature today:

....

....

....

Something I did or said which took courage:

....

....

....

Who (which part of me) will show up tomorrow to make the day even better?

- Creator / Magician ☐
- Warrior / Courage ☐
- Leader / Inspiration ☐
- Love / Authentic Self ☐

....

....

....

MORNING REFLECTION

My Power Word: " "Date:.................

Hmmm.... **How I Feel Right Now** Great

0 1 2 3 4 5 6 7 8 9 10

Today I'm grateful for:

....

....

....

My intention for the day:

....

....

....

A belief / habit to change:

....

....

....

What I can do today to get me closer to where I want to be tomorrow:

....

....

....

My daily affirmation:

....

....

....

EVENING REFLECTION

Date:..................

How I Feel Before Sleep

Hmmm.... Peaceful / Grateful

0 1 2 3 4 5 6 7 8 9 10

What did I learn today?

How I showed or received kindness today (others/self):

How I connected with nature today:

Something I did or said which took courage:

Who (which part of me) will show up tomorrow to make the day even better?

Creator / Magician

Warrior / Courage

Leader / Inspiration

Love / Authentic Self

MORNING REFLECTION

My Power Word: " "Date:.................

Hmmm.... How I Feel Right Now Great

0 1 2 3 4 5 6 7 8 9 10

Today I'm grateful for:

....

....

....

My intention for the day:

....

....

....

A belief / habit to change:

....

....

....

What I can do today to get me closer to where I want to be tomorrow:

....

....

....

My daily affirmation:

....

....

....

EVENING REFLECTION

Date:..................

How I Feel Before Sleep

Hmmm.... Peaceful / Grateful

0 1 2 3 4 5 6 7 8 9 10

What did I learn today?

....

....

....

How I showed or received kindness today (others/self):

....

....

....

How I connected with nature today:

....

....

....

Something I did or said which took courage:

....

....

....

Who (which part of me) will show up tomorrow to make the day even better?

- Creator / Magician ☐
- Warrior / Courage ☐
- Leader / Inspiration ☐
- Love / Authentic Self ☐

....

....

....

MORNING REFLECTION

My Power Word: " "Date:..................

Hmmm.... How I Feel Right Now Great

0 1 2 3 4 5 6 7 8 9 10

Today I'm grateful for:

My intention for the day:

A belief / habit to change:

What I can do today to get me closer to where I want to be tomorrow:

My daily affirmation:

EVENING REFLECTION

Date:..................

How I Feel Before Sleep

Hmmm.... Peaceful / Grateful

0 1 2 3 4 5 6 7 8 9 10

What did I learn today?

...

How I showed or received kindness today (others/self):

...

How I connected with nature today:

...

Something I did or said which took courage:

...

Who (which part of me) will show up tomorrow to make the day even better?

- Creator / Magician ☐
- Warrior / Courage ☐
- Leader / Inspiration ☐
- Love / Authentic Self ☐

focus on your senses

Date:

Colour can uplift us in many ways. Where or how can you add more colour into your daily routine and the environment around you?

I see colour...

what you wear, bathroom towels, flowers, stationery, painted nails, favourite mug, art etc

I smell colour...

herbs, flowers, bath oil, shower gel

I taste colour...

herbal teas, naturally colourful fruit and vegetables etc

I hear colour...

uplifting colourful music, meditation/hypnosis tracks, melodies, harmonics, instruments, voices, your words when you speak to others, languages, animals, the elements.... anything and everything where you can imagine colour when you hear it!

I touch colour...

clothing, bed linen, cushions, art, cooking, writing, bag, purse, flowers

I think colourful thoughts...

notice how your thinking changes when you add or change the colour of your internal thoughts

MORNING REFLECTION

My Power Word: "   " Date:..................

Hmmm.... **How I Feel Right Now** Great

0 1 2 3 4 5 6 7 8 9 10

Today I'm grateful for:

....

....

....

My intention for the day:

....

....

....

A belief / habit to change:

....

....

....

What I can do today to get me closer to where I want to be tomorrow:

....

....

....

My daily affirmation:

....

....

....

EVENING REFLECTION

Date:.................

How I Feel Before Sleep

Hmmm... Peaceful / Grateful

0 1 2 3 4 5 6 7 8 9 10

What did I learn today?

....

....

....

How I showed or received kindness today (others/self):

....

....

....

How I connected with nature today:

....

....

....

Something I did or said which took courage:

....

....

....

Who (which part of me) will show up tomorrow to make the day even better?

- Creator / Magician ☐
- Warrior / Courage ☐
- Leader / Inspiration ☐
- Love / Authentic Self ☐

....

....

....

MORNING REFLECTION

My Power Word: " "Date:..................

Hmmm.... How I Feel Right Now Great

0 1 2 3 4 5 6 7 8 9 10

Today I'm grateful for:

...

...

...

My intention for the day:

...

...

...

A belief / habit to change:

...

...

...

What I can do today to get me closer to where I want to be tomorrow:

...

...

...

My daily affirmation:

...

...

...

EVENING REFLECTION

Date:..................

How I Feel Before Sleep

Hmmm.... Peaceful / Grateful

0 1 2 3 4 5 6 7 8 9 10

What did I learn today?

...

...

...

How I showed or received kindness today (others/self):

...

...

...

How I connected with nature today:

...

...

...

Something I did or said which took courage:

...

...

...

Who (which part of me) will show up tomorrow to make the day even better?

- Creator / Magician ☐
- Warrior / Courage ☐
- Leader / Inspiration ☐
- Love / Authentic Self ☐

MORNING REFLECTION

My Power Word: " "Date:..................

Hmmm.... How I Feel Right Now Great

0 1 2 3 4 5 6 7 8 9 10

Today I'm grateful for:

....

....

....

My intention for the day:

....

....

....

A belief / habit to change:

....

....

....

What I can do today to get me closer to where I want to be tomorrow:

....

....

....

My daily affirmation:

....

....

....

EVENING REFLECTION

Date:..................

How I Feel Before Sleep

Hmmm.... Peaceful / Grateful

0 1 2 3 4 5 6 7 8 9 10

What did I learn today?

....

....

....

How I showed or received kindness today (others/self):

....

....

....

How I connected with nature today:

....

....

....

Something I did or said which took courage:

....

....

....

Who (which part of me) will show up tomorrow to make the day even better?

- Creator / Magician ☐
- Warrior / Courage ☐
- Leader / Inspiration ☐
- Love / Authentic Self ☐

....

....

....

what is not

healed or

released,

...is repeated

MORNING REFLECTION

My Power Word: "   " Date:.................

Hmmm.... How I Feel Right Now Great

0 1 2 3 4 5 6 7 8 9 10

Today I'm grateful for:

....

....

....

My intention for the day:

....

....

....

A belief / habit to change:

....

....

....

What I can do today to get me closer to where I want to be tomorrow:

....

....

....

My daily affirmation:

....

....

....

EVENING REFLECTION

Date:..................

How I Feel Before Sleep

Hmmm.... Peaceful / Grateful

0 1 2 3 4 5 6 7 8 9 10

What did I learn today?

....

....

....

How I showed or received kindness today (others/self):

....

....

....

How I connected with nature today:

....

....

....

Something I did or said which took courage:

....

....

....

Who (which part of me) will show up tomorrow to make the day even better?

- Creator / Magician ☐
- Warrior / Courage ☐
- Leader / Inspiration ☐
- Love / Authentic Self ☐

....

....

....

MORNING REFLECTION

My Power Word: "   " Date:..................

Hmmm.... How I Feel Right Now Great

0 1 2 3 4 5 6 7 8 9 10

Today I'm grateful for:

....

....

....

My intention for the day:

....

....

....

A belief / habit to change:

....

....

....

What I can do today to get me closer to where I want to be tomorrow:

....

....

....

My daily affirmation:

....

....

....

EVENING REFLECTION

Date:..................

How I Feel Before Sleep

Hmmm.... Peaceful / Grateful

0 1 2 3 4 5 6 7 8 9 10

What did I learn today?

How I showed or received kindness today (others/self):

How I connected with nature today:

Something I did or said which took courage:

Who (which part of me) will show up tomorrow to make the day even better?

Creator / Magician

Warrior / Courage

Leader / Inspiration

Love / Authentic Self

It's ALL RIGHT

When all is too much to bear
& you feel like there is no one there

Look inside & Be Strong
Find Strength - Carry On

A bird, a fly, a spider's web,
Remember, you are always led

It's All Right,
Smile, Be Brave

When we Let Go

We Know
We Grow
We Glow

Poem by
Deirdre Whitmore

© copyright Deirdre Whitmore 2024

MORNING REFLECTION

My Power Word: " "Date:..................

Hmmm.... How I Feel Right Now Great

0 1 2 3 4 5 6 7 8 9 10

Today I'm grateful for:

My intention for the day:

A belief / habit to change:

What I can do today to get me closer to where I want to be tomorrow:

My daily affirmation:

EVENING REFLECTION

Date:..................

How I Feel Before Sleep

Hmmm... Peaceful / Grateful

0 1 2 3 4 5 6 7 8 9 10

What did I learn today?

....

....

....

How I showed or received kindness today (others/self):

....

....

....

How I connected with nature today:

....

....

....

Something I did or said which took courage:

....

....

....

Who (which part of me) will show up tomorrow to make the day even better?

- [ ] Creator / Magician
- [ ] Warrior / Courage
- [ ] Leader / Inspiration
- [ ] Love / Authentic Self

....

....

....

MORNING REFLECTION

My Power Word: "   " Date:..................

Hmmm.... How I Feel Right Now Great

0 1 2 3 4 5 6 7 8 9 10

Today I'm grateful for:

....

....

....

My intention for the day:

....

....

....

A belief / habit to change:

....

....

....

What I can do today to get me closer to where I want to be tomorrow:

....

....

....

My daily affirmation:

....

....

....

EVENING REFLECTION

Date:..................

How I Feel Before Sleep

Hmmm.... Peaceful / Grateful

0 1 2 3 4 5 6 7 8 9 10

What did I learn today?

How I showed or received kindness today (others/self):

How I connected with nature today:

Something I did or said which took courage:

Who (which part of me) will show up tomorrow to make the day even better?

- Creator / Magician
- Warrior / Courage
- Leader / Inspiration
- Love / Authentic Self

MORNING REFLECTION

My Power Word: " "Date:..................

Hmmm.... How I Feel Right Now Great

0 1 2 3 4 5 6 7 8 9 10

Today I'm grateful for:

My intention for the day:

A belief / habit to change:

What I can do today to get me closer to where I want to be tomorrow:

My daily affirmation:

EVENING REFLECTION

Date:..................

How I Feel Before Sleep

Hmmm.... Peaceful / Grateful

0 1 2 3 4 5 6 7 8 9 10

What did I learn today?

....

....

....

How I showed or received kindness today (others/self):

....

....

....

How I connected with nature today:

....

....

....

Something I did or said which took courage:

....

....

....

Who (which part of me) will show up tomorrow to make the day even better?

- Creator / Magician ☐
- Warrior / Courage ☐
- Leader / Inspiration ☐
- Love / Authentic Self ☐

....

....

....

bonus day

My Power Word:

Date:

Mood/Emotion Tracker

○ ○ ○ ○ ○

SAD / LOW ⟷ HAPPY / ENERGISED

Space for Creativity

DOODLE, COLOUR, WORDS, THOUGHTS

I am Grateful for:

My Intention / Focus for today:

My Purpose / Mission:

What I GET to do today:

MORNING REFLECTION

My Power Word: "   " Date:..................

Hmmm....   How I Feel Right Now   Great

0 1 2 3 4 5 6 7 8 9 10

Today I'm grateful for:

....

....

....

My intention for the day:

....

....

....

A belief / habit to change:

....

....

....

What I can do today to get me closer to where I want to be tomorrow:

....

....

....

My daily affirmation:

....

....

....

EVENING REFLECTION

Date:..................

How I Feel Before Sleep

Hmmm.... Peaceful / Grateful

0 1 2 3 4 5 6 7 8 9 10

What did I learn today?

How I showed or received kindness today (others/self):

How I connected with nature today:

Something I did or said which took courage:

Who (which part of me) will show up tomorrow to make the day even better?

Creator / Magician

Warrior / Courage

Leader / Inspiration

Love / Authentic Self

MORNING REFLECTION

My Power Word: " " Date:..................

Hmmm.... **How I Feel Right Now** Great

0 1 2 3 4 5 6 7 8 9 10

Today I'm grateful for:

My intention for the day:

A belief / habit to change:

What I can do today to get me closer to where I want to be tomorrow:

My daily affirmation:

EVENING REFLECTION

Date:..................

How I Feel Before Sleep

Hmmm.... Peaceful / Grateful

0 1 2 3 4 5 6 7 8 9 10

What did I learn today?

....

....

....

How I showed or received kindness today (others/self):

....

....

....

How I connected with nature today:

....

....

....

Something I did or said which took courage:

....

....

....

Who (which part of me) will show up tomorrow to make the day even better?

Creator / Magician ☐ ....

Warrior / Courage ☐ ....

Leader / Inspiration ☐ ....

Love / Authentic Self ☐

MORNING REFLECTION

My Power Word: "   " Date:..................

Hmmm....   How I Feel Right Now   Great

0 1 2 3 4 5 6 7 8 9 10

Today I'm grateful for:

....

....

....

My intention for the day:

....

....

....

A belief / habit to change:

....

....

....

What I can do today to get me closer to where I want to be tomorrow:

....

....

....

My daily affirmation:

....

....

....

EVENING REFLECTION

Date:..................

How I Feel Before Sleep

Hmmm.... Peaceful / Grateful

0 1 2 3 4 5 6 7 8 9 10

What did I learn today?

How I showed or received kindness today (others/self):

How I connected with nature today:

Something I did or said which took courage:

Who (which part of me) will show up tomorrow to make the day even better?

Creator / Magician ☐

Warrior / Courage ☐

Leader / Inspiration ☐

Love / Authentic Self ☐

Sometimes it's the *smallest* things that make the *biggest* difference

MORNING REFLECTION

My Power Word: "   "Date:..................

Hmmm....   How I Feel Right Now   Great

0 1 2 3 4 5 6 7 8 9 10

Today I'm grateful for:

....

....

....

My intention for the day:

....

....

....

A belief / habit to change:

....

....

....

What I can do today to get me closer to where I want to be tomorrow:

....

....

....

My daily affirmation:

....

....

....

EVENING REFLECTION

Date:.................

How I Feel Before Sleep

Hmmm.... Peaceful / Grateful

0 1 2 3 4 5 6 7 8 9 10

What did I learn today?

....

....

....

How I showed or received kindness today (others/self):

....

....

....

How I connected with nature today:

....

....

....

Something I did or said which took courage:

....

....

....

Who (which part of me) will show up tomorrow to make the day even better?

- Creator / Magician ☐
- Warrior / Courage ☐
- Leader / Inspiration ☐
- Love / Authentic Self ☐

....

....

....

MORNING REFLECTION

My Power Word: " "Date:..................

Hmmm.... How I Feel Right Now Great

0 1 2 3 4 5 6 7 8 9 10

Today I'm grateful for:

My intention for the day:

A belief / habit to change:

What I can do today to get me closer to where I want to be tomorrow:

My daily affirmation:

EVENING REFLECTION

Date:..................

How I Feel Before Sleep

Hmmm.... 0 1 2 3 4 5 6 7 8 9 10 Peaceful / Grateful

What did I learn today?

How I showed or received kindness today (others/self):

How I connected with nature today:

Something I did or said which took courage:

Who (which part of me) will show up tomorrow to make the day even better?

- Creator / Magician ☐
- Warrior / Courage ☐
- Leader / Inspiration ☐
- Love / Authentic Self ☐

MORNING REFLECTION

My Power Word: "   "Date:..................

Hmmm....   How I Feel Right Now   Great

0 1 2 3 4 5 6 7 8 9 10

Today I'm grateful for:

My intention for the day:

A belief / habit to change:

What I can do today to get me closer to where I want to be tomorrow:

My daily affirmation:

EVENING REFLECTION

Date:.................

How I Feel Before Sleep

Hmmm.... Peaceful / Grateful

0 1 2 3 4 5 6 7 8 9 10

What did I learn today?

....

....

....

How I showed or received kindness today (others/self):

....

....

....

How I connected with nature today:

....

....

....

Something I did or said which took courage:

....

....

....

Who (which part of me) will show up tomorrow to make the day even better?

- Creator / Magician ☐
- Warrior / Courage ☐
- Leader / Inspiration ☐
- Love / Authentic Self ☐

....

....

....

MORNING REFLECTION

My Power Word: " "Date:..................

Hmmm.... **How I Feel Right Now** Great

0 1 2 3 4 5 6 7 8 9 10

Today I'm grateful for:

My intention for the day:

A belief / habit to change:

What I can do today to get me closer to where I want to be tomorrow:

My daily affirmation:

EVENING REFLECTION

Date:..................

How I Feel Before Sleep

Hmmm.... Peaceful / Grateful

0 1 2 3 4 5 6 7 8 9 10

What did I learn today?

....

....

....

How I showed or received kindness today (others/self):

....

....

....

How I connected with nature today:

....

....

....

Something I did or said which took courage:

....

....

....

Who (which part of me) will show up tomorrow to make the day even better?

- Creator / Magician ☐
- Warrior / Courage ☐
- Leader / Inspiration ☐
- Love / Authentic Self ☐

....

....

....

bonus day

My Power Word:

Date:

Mood/Emotion Tracker

○ ○ ○ ○ ○

SAD / LOW ⟷ HAPPY / ENERGISED

Space for Creativity

DOODLE, COLOUR, WORDS, THOUGHTS

I am Grateful for:

My Intention / Focus for today:

My Purpose / Mission:

What I GET to do today:

MORNING REFLECTION

My Power Word: " " Date:..................

Hmmm.... How I Feel Right Now Great

0 1 2 3 4 5 6 7 8 9 10

Today I'm grateful for:

My intention for the day:

A belief / habit to change:

What I can do today to get me closer to where I want to be tomorrow:

My daily affirmation:

EVENING REFLECTION

Date:..................

How I Feel Before Sleep

Hmmm.... Peaceful / Grateful

0 1 2 3 4 5 6 7 8 9 10

What did I learn today?

....

....

....

How I showed or received kindness today (others/self):

....

....

....

How I connected with nature today:

....

....

....

Something I did or said which took courage:

....

....

....

Who (which part of me) will show up tomorrow to make the day even better?

- Creator / Magician ☐
- Warrior / Courage ☐
- Leader / Inspiration ☐
- Love / Authentic Self ☐

....

....

....

MORNING REFLECTION

My Power Word: " " Date:.................

Hmmm.... How I Feel Right Now Great

0 1 2 3 4 5 6 7 8 9 10

Today I'm grateful for:

...

...

...

My intention for the day:

...

...

...

A belief / habit to change:

...

...

...

What I can do today to get me closer to where I want to be tomorrow:

...

...

...

My daily affirmation:

...

...

...

EVENING REFLECTION

Date:..................

How I Feel Before Sleep

Hmmm.... Peaceful / Grateful

0 1 2 3 4 5 6 7 8 9 10

What did I learn today?

How I showed or received kindness today (others/self):

How I connected with nature today:

Something I did or said which took courage:

Who (which part of me) will show up tomorrow to make the day even better?

Creator / Magician ☐

Warrior / Courage ☐

Leader / Inspiration ☐

Love / Authentic Self ☐

MORNING REFLECTION

My Power Word: "   " Date:.................

Hmmm....   How I Feel Right Now   Great

0 1 2 3 4 5 6 7 8 9 10

Today I'm grateful for:

....

....

....

My intention for the day:

....

....

....

A belief / habit to change:

....

....

....

What I can do today to get me closer to where I want to be tomorrow:

....

....

....

My daily affirmation:

....

....

....

EVENING REFLECTION

Date:..................

How I Feel Before Sleep

Hmmm.... Peaceful / Grateful

0 1 2 3 4 5 6 7 8 9 10

What did I learn today?

How I showed or received kindness today (others/self):

How I connected with nature today:

Something I did or said which took courage:

Who (which part of me) will show up tomorrow to make the day even better?

- Creator / Magician ☐
- Warrior / Courage ☐
- Leader / Inspiration ☐
- Love / Authentic Self ☐

MORNING REFLECTION

My Power Word: " " Date:.................

Hmmm.... How I Feel Right Now Great

0 1 2 3 4 5 6 7 8 9 10

Today I'm grateful for:

My intention for the day:

A belief / habit to change:

What I can do today to get me closer to where I want to be tomorrow:

My daily affirmation:

EVENING REFLECTION

Date:..................

How I Feel Before Sleep

Hmmm.... Peaceful / Grateful

0 1 2 3 4 5 6 7 8 9 10

What did I learn today?

How I showed or received kindness today (others/self):

How I connected with nature today:

Something I did or said which took courage:

Who (which part of me) will show up tomorrow to make the day even better?

Creator / Magician

Warrior / Courage

Leader / Inspiration

Love / Authentic Self

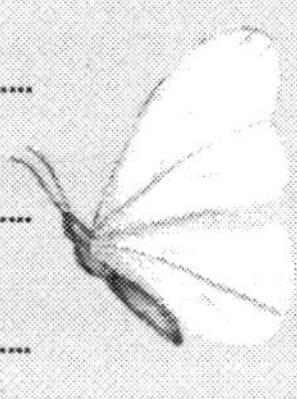

MORNING REFLECTION

My Power Word: " " Date:..................

Hmmm.... How I Feel Right Now Great

0 1 2 3 4 5 6 7 8 9 10

Today I'm grateful for:

....

....

....

My intention for the day:

....

....

....

A belief / habit to change:

....

....

....

What I can do today to get me closer to where I want to be tomorrow:

....

....

....

My daily affirmation:

....

....

....

EVENING REFLECTION

Date:..................

How I Feel Before Sleep

Hmmm.... Peaceful / Grateful

0 1 2 3 4 5 6 7 8 9 10

What did I learn today?

How I showed or received kindness today (others/self):

How I connected with nature today:

Something I did or said which took courage:

Who (which part of me) will show up tomorrow to make the day even better?

- Creator / Magician ☐
- Warrior / Courage ☐
- Leader / Inspiration ☐
- Love / Authentic Self ☐

MORNING REFLECTION

My Power Word: " " Date:.................

Hmmm.... **How I Feel Right Now** Great

0 1 2 3 4 5 6 7 8 9 10

Today I'm grateful for:

....

....

....

My intention for the day:

....

....

....

A belief / habit to change:

....

....

....

What I can do today to get me closer to where I want to be tomorrow:

....

....

....

My daily affirmation:

....

....

....

EVENING REFLECTION

Date:..................

How I Feel Before Sleep

Hmmm.... 0 1 2 3 4 5 6 7 8 9 10 Peaceful / Grateful

What did I learn today?

....

....

....

How I showed or received kindness today (others/self):

....

....

....

How I connected with nature today:

....

....

....

Something I did or said which took courage:

....

....

....

Who (which part of me) will show up tomorrow to make the day even better?

- Creator / Magician ☐ ....
- Warrior / Courage ☐ ....
- Leader / Inspiration ☐ ....
- Love / Authentic Self ☐

MORNING REFLECTION

My Power Word: " " Date:..................

Hmmm.... How I Feel Right Now Great

0 1 2 3 4 5 6 7 8 9 10

Today I'm grateful for:

....

....

....

My intention for the day:

....

....

....

A belief / habit to change:

....

....

....

What I can do today to get me closer to where I want to be tomorrow:

....

....

....

My daily affirmation:

....

....

....

EVENING REFLECTION

Date:..................

How I Feel Before Sleep

Hmmm.... Peaceful / Grateful

0 1 2 3 4 5 6 7 8 9 10

What did I learn today?

How I showed or received kindness today (others/self):

How I connected with nature today:

Something I did or said which took courage:

Who (which part of me) will show up tomorrow to make the day even better?

Creator / Magician

Warrior / Courage

Leader / Inspiration

Love / Authentic Self

always believe something wonderful is going to happen...

MORNING REFLECTION

My Power Word: "   "Date:..................

Hmmm....   How I Feel Right Now   Great

0 1 2 3 4 5 6 7 8 9 10

Today I'm grateful for:

....

....

....

My intention for the day:

....

....

....

A belief / habit to change:

....

....

....

What I can do today to get me closer to where I want to be tomorrow:

....

....

....

My daily affirmation:

....

....

....

EVENING REFLECTION

Date:.................

How I Feel Before Sleep

Hmmm.... Peaceful / Grateful

0 1 2 3 4 5 6 7 8 9 10

What did I learn today?

....

....

....

How I showed or received kindness today (others/self):

....

....

....

How I connected with nature today:

....

....

....

Something I did or said which took courage:

....

....

....

Who (which part of me) will show up tomorrow to make the day even better?

- Creator / Magician ☐
- Warrior / Courage ☐
- Leader / Inspiration ☐
- Love / Authentic Self ☐

....

....

....

MORNING REFLECTION

My Power Word: " "Date:..................

Hmmm.... How I Feel Right Now Great

0 1 2 3 4 5 6 7 8 9 10

Today I'm grateful for:

....

....

....

My intention for the day:

....

....

....

A belief / habit to change:

....

....

....

What I can do today to get me closer to where I want to be tomorrow:

....

....

....

My daily affirmation:

....

....

....

EVENING REFLECTION

Date:..................

How I Feel Before Sleep

Hmmm.... Peaceful / Grateful

0 1 2 3 4 5 6 7 8 9 10

What did I learn today?

How I showed or received kindness today (others/self):

How I connected with nature today:

Something I did or said which took courage:

Who (which part of me) will show up tomorrow to make the day even better?

- Creator / Magician ☐
- Warrior / Courage ☐
- Leader / Inspiration ☐
- Love / Authentic Self ☐

MORNING REFLECTION

My Power Word: "   " Date:..................

Hmmm.... How I Feel Right Now Great

0 1 2 3 4 5 6 7 8 9 10

Today I'm grateful for:

....

....

....

My intention for the day:

....

....

....

A belief / habit to change:

....

....

....

What I can do today to get me closer to where I want to be tomorrow:

....

....

....

My daily affirmation:

....

....

....

EVENING REFLECTION

Date:..................

How I Feel Before Sleep

Hmmm.... Peaceful / Grateful

0 1 2 3 4 5 6 7 8 9 10

What did I learn today?

....

....

....

How I showed or received kindness today (others/self):

....

....

....

How I connected with nature today:

....

....

....

Something I did or said which took courage:

....

....

....

Who (which part of me) will show up tomorrow to make the day even better?

- [ ] Creator / Magician
- [ ] Warrior / Courage
- [ ] Leader / Inspiration
- [ ] Love / Authentic Self

....

....

....

bonus day

My Power Word:

Date:

Mood/Emotion Tracker

○ ○ ○ ○ ○

SAD / LOW ⟷ HAPPY / ENERGISED

Space for Creativity

DOODLE, COLOUR, WORDS, THOUGHTS

I am Grateful for:

My Intention / Focus for today:

My Purpose / Mission:

What I GET to do today:

MORNING REFLECTION

My Power Word: "   "Date:.................

Hmmm....   How I Feel Right Now   Great

0 1 2 3 4 5 6 7 8 9 10

Today I'm grateful for:

....

....

....

My intention for the day:

....

....

....

A belief / habit to change:

....

....

....

What I can do today to get me closer to where I want to be tomorrow:

....

....

....

My daily affirmation:

....

....

....

EVENING REFLECTION

Date:..................

How I Feel Before Sleep

Hmmm.... Peaceful / Grateful

0 1 2 3 4 5 6 7 8 9 10

What did I learn today?

....

....

....

How I showed or received kindness today (others/self):

....

....

....

How I connected with nature today:

....

....

....

Something I did or said which took courage:

....

....

....

Who (which part of me) will show up tomorrow to make the day even better?

Creator / Magician ☐ ....

Warrior / Courage ☐ ....

Leader / Inspiration ☐ ....

Love / Authentic Self ☐

MORNING REFLECTION

My Power Word: " "Date:..................

Hmmm.... How I Feel Right Now Great

0 1 2 3 4 5 6 7 8 9 10

Today I'm grateful for:

My intention for the day:

A belief / habit to change:

What I can do today to get me closer to where I want to be tomorrow:

My daily affirmation:

EVENING REFLECTION

Date:..................

How I Feel Before Sleep

Hmmm.... Peaceful / Grateful

0 1 2 3 4 5 6 7 8 9 10

What did I learn today?

How I showed or received kindness today (others/self):

How I connected with nature today:

Something I did or said which took courage:

Who (which part of me) will show up tomorrow to make the day even better?

Creator / Magician

Warrior / Courage

Leader / Inspiration

Love / Authentic Self

MORNING REFLECTION

My Power Word: " "Date:..................

Hmmm.... How I Feel Right Now Great

0 1 2 3 4 5 6 7 8 9 10

Today I'm grateful for:

....

....

....

My intention for the day:

....

....

....

A belief / habit to change:

....

....

....

What I can do today to get me closer to where I want to be tomorrow:

....

....

....

My daily affirmation:

....

....

....

EVENING REFLECTION

Date:..................

How I Feel Before Sleep

Hmmm.... Peaceful / Grateful

0 1 2 3 4 5 6 7 8 9 10

What did I learn today?

....

....

....

How I showed or received kindness today (others/self):

....

....

....

How I connected with nature today:

....

....

....

Something I did or said which took courage:

....

....

....

Who (which part of me) will show up tomorrow to make the day even better?

- Creator / Magician ☐
- Warrior / Courage ☐
- Leader / Inspiration ☐
- Love / Authentic Self ☐

....

....

....

It's not always *their* business... and it's not always *your* business...

MORNING REFLECTION

My Power Word: "   "Date:..................

Hmmm.... How I Feel Right Now Great

0 1 2 3 4 5 6 7 8 9 10

Today I'm grateful for:

My intention for the day:

A belief / habit to change:

What I can do today to get me closer to where I want to be tomorrow:

My daily affirmation:

EVENING REFLECTION

Date:..................

How I Feel Before Sleep

Hmmm.... Peaceful / Grateful

0 1 2 3 4 5 6 7 8 9 10

What did I learn today?

How I showed or received kindness today (others/self):

How I connected with nature today:

Something I did or said which took courage:

Who (which part of me) will show up tomorrow to make the day even better?

- Creator / Magician ☐
- Warrior / Courage ☐
- Leader / Inspiration ☐
- Love / Authentic Self ☐

MORNING REFLECTION

My Power Word: " "Date:..................

Hmmm.... How I Feel Right Now Great

0 1 2 3 4 5 6 7 8 9 10

Today I'm grateful for:

My intention for the day:

A belief / habit to change:

What I can do today to get me closer to where I want to be tomorrow:

My daily affirmation:

EVENING REFLECTION

Date:..................

How I Feel Before Sleep

Hmmm.... Peaceful / Grateful

0 1 2 3 4 5 6 7 8 9 10

What did I learn today?

....

....

....

How I showed or received kindness today (others/self):

....

....

....

How I connected with nature today:

....

....

....

Something I did or said which took courage:

....

....

....

Who (which part of me) will show up tomorrow to make the day even better?

- Creator / Magician ☐
- Warrior / Courage ☐
- Leader / Inspiration ☐
- Love / Authentic Self ☐

....

....

....

MORNING REFLECTION

My Power Word: "   "Date:..................

Hmmm....   How I Feel Right Now   Great

0 1 2 3 4 5 6 7 8 9 10

Today I'm grateful for:

....

....

....

My intention for the day:

....

....

....

A belief / habit to change:

....

....

....

What I can do today to get me closer to where I want to be tomorrow:

....

....

....

My daily affirmation:

....

....

....

EVENING REFLECTION

Date:..................

How I Feel Before Sleep

Hmmm.... 0 1 2 3 4 5 6 7 8 9 10 Peaceful / Grateful

What did I learn today?

....

....

....

How I showed or received kindness today (others/self):

....

....

....

How I connected with nature today:

....

....

....

Something I did or said which took courage:

....

....

....

Who (which part of me) will show up tomorrow to make the day even better?

Creator / Magician ☐

Warrior / Courage ☐

Leader / Inspiration ☐

Love / Authentic Self ☐

....

....

....

MORNING REFLECTION

My Power Word: " **"Date:.................**

Hmmm.... **How I Feel Right Now** Great

0 1 2 3 4 5 6 7 8 9 10

Today I'm grateful for:

My intention for the day:

A belief / habit to change:

What I can do today to get me closer to where I want to be tomorrow:

My daily affirmation:

EVENING REFLECTION

Date:..................

How I Feel Before Sleep

Hmmm.... Peaceful / Grateful

0 1 2 3 4 5 6 7 8 9 10

What did I learn today?

How I showed or received kindness today (others/self):

How I connected with nature today:

Something I did or said which took courage:

Who (which part of me) will show up tomorrow to make the day even better?

Creator / Magician ☐

Warrior / Courage ☐

Leader / Inspiration ☐

Love / Authentic Self ☐

MORNING REFLECTION

My Power Word: "   "Date:..................

Hmmm....   How I Feel Right Now   Great

0 1 2 3 4 5 6 7 8 9 10

Today I'm grateful for:

My intention for the day:

A belief / habit to change:

What I can do today to get me closer to where I want to be tomorrow:

My daily affirmation:

EVENING REFLECTION

Date:..................

How I Feel Before Sleep

Hmmm.... Peaceful / Grateful

0 1 2 3 4 5 6 7 8 9 10

What did I learn today?

....

....

....

How I showed or received kindness today (others/self):

....

....

....

How I connected with nature today:

....

....

....

Something I did or said which took courage:

....

....

....

Who (which part of me) will show up tomorrow to make the day even better?

- Creator / Magician ☐
- Warrior / Courage ☐
- Leader / Inspiration ☐
- Love / Authentic Self ☐

....

....

....

MORNING REFLECTION

My Power Word: "   "Date:..................

Hmmm....   How I Feel Right Now   Great

0 1 2 3 4 5 6 7 8 9 10

Today I'm grateful for:

....

....

....

My intention for the day:

....

....

....

A belief / habit to change:

....

....

....

What I can do today to get me closer to where I want to be tomorrow:

....

....

....

My daily affirmation:

....

....

....

EVENING REFLECTION

Date:..................

How I Feel Before Sleep

Hmmm... 0 1 2 3 4 5 6 7 8 9 10 Peaceful / Grateful

What did I learn today?

....

....

....

How I showed or received kindness today (others/self):

....

....

....

How I connected with nature today:

....

....

....

Something I did or said which took courage:

....

....

....

Who (which part of me) will show up tomorrow to make the day even better?

- [ ] Creator / Magician
- [ ] Warrior / Courage
- [ ] Leader / Inspiration
- [ ] Love / Authentic Self

....

....

....

MORNING REFLECTION

My Power Word: "   "Date:..................

Hmmm....   How I Feel Right Now   Great

0 1 2 3 4 5 6 7 8 9 10

Today I'm grateful for:

....

....

....

My intention for the day:

....

....

....

A belief / habit to change:

....

....

....

What I can do today to get me closer to where I want to be tomorrow:

....

....

....

My daily affirmation:

....

....

....

EVENING REFLECTION

Date:..................

How I Feel Before Sleep

Hmmm.... Peaceful / Grateful

0 1 2 3 4 5 6 7 8 9 10

What did I learn today?

....

....

....

How I showed or received kindness today (others/self):

....

....

....

How I connected with nature today:

....

....

....

Something I did or said which took courage:

....

....

....

Who (which part of me) will show up tomorrow to make the day even better?

- Creator / Magician ☐
- Warrior / Courage ☐
- Leader / Inspiration ☐
- Love / Authentic Self ☐

....

....

....

MORNING REFLECTION

My Power Word: "   " Date:..................

Hmmm....   How I Feel Right Now   Great

0 1 2 3 4 5 6 7 8 9 10

Today I'm grateful for:

....

....

....

My intention for the day:

....

....

....

A belief / habit to change:

....

....

....

What I can do today to get me closer to where I want to be tomorrow:

....

....

....

My daily affirmation:

....

....

....

EVENING REFLECTION

Date:.................

How I Feel Before Sleep

Hmmm.... Peaceful / Grateful

0 1 2 3 4 5 6 7 8 9 10

What did I learn today?

....

....

....

How I showed or received kindness today (others/self):

....

....

....

How I connected with nature today:

....

....

....

Something I did or said which took courage:

....

....

....

Who (which part of me) will show up tomorrow to make the day even better?

- Creator / Magician ☐ ....
- Warrior / Courage ☐ ....
- Leader / Inspiration ☐ ....
- Love / Authentic Self ☐

MORNING REFLECTION

My Power Word: "   "Date:..................

Hmmm....   How I Feel Right Now   Great

0 1 2 3 4 5 6 7 8 9 10

Today I'm grateful for:

....

....

....

My intention for the day:

....

....

....

A belief / habit to change:

....

....

....

What I can do today to get me closer to where I want to be tomorrow:

....

....

....

My daily affirmation:

....

....

....

EVENING REFLECTION

Date:..................

How I Feel Before Sleep

Hmmm... Peaceful / Grateful

0 1 2 3 4 5 6 7 8 9 10

What did I learn today?

....

....

....

How I showed or received kindness today (others/self):

....

....

....

How I connected with nature today:

....

....

....

Something I did or said which took courage:

....

....

....

Who (which part of me) will show up tomorrow to make the day even better?

- [ ] Creator / Magician
- [ ] Warrior / Courage
- [ ] Leader / Inspiration
- [ ] Love / Authentic Self

....

....

....

MORNING REFLECTION

My Power Word: "   " Date:..................

Hmmm....   How I Feel Right Now   Great

0 1 2 3 4 5 6 7 8 9 10

Today I'm grateful for:

....

....

....

My intention for the day:

....

....

....

A belief / habit to change:

....

....

....

What I can do today to get me closer to where I want to be tomorrow:

....

....

....

My daily affirmation:

....

....

....

EVENING REFLECTION

Date:..................

How I Feel Before Sleep

Hmmm.... Peaceful / Grateful

0 1 2 3 4 5 6 7 8 9 10

What did I learn today?

....

....

....

How I showed or received kindness today (others/self):

....

....

....

How I connected with nature today:

....

....

....

Something I did or said which took courage:

....

....

....

Who (which part of me) will show up tomorrow to make the day even better?

Creator / Magician ☐ ....

Warrior / Courage ☐ ....

Leader / Inspiration ☐ ....

Love / Authentic Self ☐

When We Are Kind To Ourselves, Our Kindness Radiates To Others

MORNING REFLECTION

My Power Word: " "Date:.................

Hmmm.... How I Feel Right Now Great

0 1 2 3 4 5 6 7 8 9 10

Today I'm grateful for:

My intention for the day:

A belief / habit to change:

What I can do today to get me closer to where I want to be tomorrow:

My daily affirmation:

EVENING REFLECTION

Date:..................

How I Feel Before Sleep

Hmmm.... Peaceful / Grateful

0 1 2 3 4 5 6 7 8 9 10

What did I learn today?

....

....

....

How I showed or received kindness today (others/self):

....

....

....

How I connected with nature today:

....

....

....

Something I did or said which took courage:

....

....

....

Who (which part of me) will show up tomorrow to make the day even better?

- [ ] Creator / Magician
- [ ] Warrior / Courage
- [ ] Leader / Inspiration
- [ ] Love / Authentic Self

....

....

....

MORNING REFLECTION

My Power Word: ” “Date:.................

Hmmm.... **How I Feel Right Now** Great

0 1 2 3 4 5 6 7 8 9 10

Today I'm grateful for:

My intention for the day:

A belief / habit to change:

What I can do today to get me closer to where I want to be tomorrow:

My daily affirmation:

EVENING REFLECTION

Date:..................

How I Feel Before Sleep

Hmmm.... Peaceful / Grateful

0 1 2 3 4 5 6 7 8 9 10

What did I learn today?

....

....

....

How I showed or received kindness today (others/self):

....

....

....

How I connected with nature today:

....

....

....

Something I did or said which took courage:

....

....

....

Who (which part of me) will show up tomorrow to make the day even better?

Creator / Magician ☐

Warrior / Courage ☐

Leader / Inspiration ☐

Love / Authentic Self ☐

....

....

....

MORNING REFLECTION

My Power Word: " "Date:..................

Hmmm.... How I Feel Right Now Great

0 1 2 3 4 5 6 7 8 9 10

Today I'm grateful for:

....

....

....

My intention for the day:

....

....

....

A belief / habit to change:

....

....

....

What I can do today to get me closer to where I want to be tomorrow:

....

....

....

My daily affirmation:

....

....

....

EVENING REFLECTION

Date:..................

How I Feel Before Sleep

Hmmm.... Peaceful / Grateful

0 1 2 3 4 5 6 7 8 9 10

What did I learn today?

How I showed or received kindness today (others/self):

How I connected with nature today:

Something I did or said which took courage:

Who (which part of me) will show up tomorrow to make the day even better?

Creator / Magician ☐

Warrior / Courage ☐

Leader / Inspiration ☐

Love / Authentic Self ☐

bonus day

My Power Word:

Date:

Mood/Emotion Tracker

○ ○ ○ ○ ○

SAD / LOW ⟷ HAPPY / ENERGISED

Space for Creativity

DOODLE, COLOUR, WORDS, THOUGHTS

I am Grateful for:

My Intention / Focus for today:

My Purpose / Mission:

What I GET to do today:

MORNING REFLECTION

My Power Word: " "Date:..................

Hmmm.... How I Feel Right Now Great

0 1 2 3 4 5 6 7 8 9 10

Today I'm grateful for:

...

...

...

My intention for the day:

...

...

...

A belief / habit to change:

...

...

...

What I can do today to get me closer to where I want to be tomorrow:

...

...

...

My daily affirmation:

...

...

...

EVENING REFLECTION

Date:..................

How I Feel Before Sleep

Hmmm.... Peaceful / Grateful

0 1 2 3 4 5 6 7 8 9 10

What did I learn today?

....

....

....

How I showed or received kindness today (others/self):

....

....

....

How I connected with nature today:

....

....

....

Something I did or said which took courage:

....

....

....

Who (which part of me) will show up tomorrow to make the day even better?

- Creator / Magician ☐
- Warrior / Courage ☐
- Leader / Inspiration ☐
- Love / Authentic Self ☐

....

....

....

MORNING REFLECTION

My Power Word: "   " Date:..................

Hmmm....   **How I Feel Right Now**   Great

0 1 2 3 4 5 6 7 8 9 10

Today I'm grateful for:

....

....

....

My intention for the day:

....

....

....

A belief / habit to change:

....

....

....

What I can do today to get me closer to where I want to be tomorrow:

....

....

....

My daily affirmation:

....

....

....

EVENING REFLECTION

Date:..................

How I Feel Before Sleep

Hmmm.... Peaceful / Grateful

0 1 2 3 4 5 6 7 8 9 10

What did I learn today?

....

....

....

How I showed or received kindness today (others/self):

....

....

....

How I connected with nature today:

....

....

....

Something I did or said which took courage:

....

....

....

Who (which part of me) will show up tomorrow to make the day even better?

- Creator / Magician ☐
- Warrior / Courage ☐
- Leader / Inspiration ☐
- Love / Authentic Self ☐

....

....

....

MORNING REFLECTION

My Power Word: "   "Date:.................

Hmmm....   How I Feel Right Now   Great

0 1 2 3 4 5 6 7 8 9 10

Today I'm grateful for:

....

....

....

My intention for the day:

....

....

....

A belief / habit to change:

....

....

....

What I can do today to get me closer to where I want to be tomorrow:

....

....

....

My daily affirmation:

....

....

....

EVENING REFLECTION

Date:..................

How I Feel Before Sleep

Hmmm.... Peaceful / Grateful

0 1 2 3 4 5 6 7 8 9 10

What did I learn today?

....

....

....

How I showed or received kindness today (others/self):

....

....

....

How I connected with nature today:

....

....

....

Something I did or said which took courage:

....

....

....

Who (which part of me) will show up tomorrow to make the day even better?

- Creator / Magician ☐
- Warrior / Courage ☐
- Leader / Inspiration ☐
- Love / Authentic Self ☐

....

....

....

MORNING REFLECTION

My Power Word: " "Date:..................

Hmmm.... **How I Feel Right Now** Great

0 1 2 3 4 5 6 7 8 9 10

Today I'm grateful for:

My intention for the day:

A belief / habit to change:

What I can do today to get me closer to where I want to be tomorrow:

My daily affirmation:

EVENING REFLECTION

Date:..................

How I Feel Before Sleep

Hmmm.... Peaceful / Grateful

0 1 2 3 4 5 6 7 8 9 10

What did I learn today?

....

....

....

How I showed or received kindness today (others/self):

....

....

....

How I connected with nature today:

....

....

....

Something I did or said which took courage:

....

....

....

Who (which part of me) will show up tomorrow to make the day even better?

Creator / Magician ☐ ....

Warrior / Courage ☐ ....

Leader / Inspiration ☐ ....

Love / Authentic Self ☐

MORNING REFLECTION

My Power Word: "   "Date:..................

Hmmm....   How I Feel Right Now   Great

0 1 2 3 4 5 6 7 8 9 10

Today I'm grateful for:

....

....

....

My intention for the day:

....

....

....

A belief / habit to change:

....

....

....

What I can do today to get me closer to where I want to be tomorrow:

....

....

....

My daily affirmation:

....

....

....

EVENING REFLECTION

Date:..................

How I Feel Before Sleep

Hmmm... Peaceful / Grateful

0 1 2 3 4 5 6 7 8 9 10

What did I learn today?

How I showed or received kindness today (others/self):

How I connected with nature today:

Something I did or said which took courage:

Who (which part of me) will show up tomorrow to make the day even better?

- Creator / Magician ☐
- Warrior / Courage ☐
- Leader / Inspiration ☐
- Love / Authentic Self ☐

MORNING REFLECTION

My Power Word: "   "Date:.................

Hmmm....   How I Feel Right Now   Great

0 1 2 3 4 5 6 7 8 9 10

Today I'm grateful for:

....

....

....

My intention for the day:

....

....

....

A belief / habit to change:

....

....

....

What I can do today to get me closer to where I want to be tomorrow:

....

....

....

My daily affirmation:

....

....

....

EVENING REFLECTION

Date:..................

How I Feel Before Sleep

Hmmm.... Peaceful / Grateful

0 1 2 3 4 5 6 7 8 9 10

What did I learn today?

....

....

....

How I showed or received kindness today (others/self):

....

....

....

How I connected with nature today:

....

....

....

Something I did or said which took courage:

....

....

....

Who (which part of me) will show up tomorrow to make the day even better?

- Creator / Magician ☐
- Warrior / Courage ☐
- Leader / Inspiration ☐
- Love / Authentic Self ☐

....

....

....

MORNING REFLECTION

My Power Word: "   "Date:..................

Hmmm....   How I Feel Right Now   Great

0 1 2 3 4 5 6 7 8 9 10

Today I'm grateful for:

....

....

....

My intention for the day:

....

....

....

A belief / habit to change:

....

....

....

What I can do today to get me closer to where I want to be tomorrow:

....

....

....

My daily affirmation:

....

....

....

EVENING REFLECTION

Date:..................

How I Feel Before Sleep

Hmmm.... Peaceful / Grateful

0 1 2 3 4 5 6 7 8 9 10

What did I learn today?

....

....

....

How I showed or received kindness today (others/self):

....

....

....

How I connected with nature today:

....

....

....

Something I did or said which took courage:

....

....

....

Who (which part of me) will show up tomorrow to make the day even better?

- [ ] Creator / Magician
- [ ] Warrior / Courage
- [ ] Leader / Inspiration
- [ ] Love / Authentic Self

....

....

....

SMILE at everyone today because they may just carry on your smile to someone else...

Now imagine a world that smiles back at you too

MORNING REFLECTION

My Power Word: "   " Date:.................

Hmmm.... How I Feel Right Now Great

0 1 2 3 4 5 6 7 8 9 10

Today I'm grateful for:

....

....

....

My intention for the day:

....

....

....

A belief / habit to change:

....

....

....

What I can do today to get me closer to where I want to be tomorrow:

....

....

....

My daily affirmation:

....

....

....

EVENING REFLECTION

Date:..................

How I Feel Before Sleep

Hmmm... Peaceful / Grateful

0 1 2 3 4 5 6 7 8 9 10

What did I learn today?

How I showed or received kindness today (others/self):

How I connected with nature today:

Something I did or said which took courage:

Who (which part of me) will show up tomorrow to make the day even better?

Creator / Magician ☐

Warrior / Courage ☐

Leader / Inspiration ☐

Love / Authentic Self ☐

MORNING REFLECTION

My Power Word: " "Date:..................

Hmmm.... How I Feel Right Now Great

0 1 2 3 4 5 6 7 8 9 10

Today I'm grateful for:

....

....

....

My intention for the day:

....

....

....

A belief / habit to change:

....

....

....

What I can do today to get me closer to where I want to be tomorrow:

....

....

....

My daily affirmation:

....

....

....

EVENING REFLECTION

Date:..................

How I Feel Before Sleep

Hmmm.... Peaceful / Grateful

0 1 2 3 4 5 6 7 8 9 10

What did I learn today?

....

....

....

How I showed or received kindness today (others/self):

....

....

....

How I connected with nature today:

....

....

....

Something I did or said which took courage:

....

....

....

Who (which part of me) will show up tomorrow to make the day even better?

- [ ] Creator / Magician
- [ ] Warrior / Courage
- [ ] Leader / Inspiration
- [ ] Love / Authentic Self

....

....

....

MORNING REFLECTION

My Power Word: "   "Date:..................

Hmmm....   How I Feel Right Now   Great

0   1   2   3   4   5   6   7   8   9   10

Today I'm grateful for:

....

....

....

My intention for the day:

....

....

....

A belief / habit to change:

....

....

....

What I can do today to get me closer to where I want to be tomorrow:

....

....

....

My daily affirmation:

....

....

....

EVENING REFLECTION

Date:..................

How I Feel Before Sleep

Hmmm.... Peaceful / Grateful

0 1 2 3 4 5 6 7 8 9 10

What did I learn today?

....

....

....

How I showed or received kindness today (others/self):

....

....

....

How I connected with nature today:

....

....

....

Something I did or said which took courage:

....

....

....

Who (which part of me) will show up tomorrow to make the day even better?

- Creator / Magician ☐ ....
- Warrior / Courage ☐ ....
- Leader / Inspiration ☐ ....
- Love / Authentic Self ☐

MORNING REFLECTION

My Power Word: "   "Date:.................

Hmmm.... How I Feel Right Now Great

0 1 2 3 4 5 6 7 8 9 10

Today I'm grateful for:

....

....

....

My intention for the day:

....

....

....

A belief / habit to change:

....

....

....

What I can do today to get me closer to where I want to be tomorrow:

....

....

....

My daily affirmation:

....

....

....

EVENING REFLECTION

Date:..................

How I Feel Before Sleep

Hmmm.... Peaceful / Grateful

0 1 2 3 4 5 6 7 8 9 10

What did I learn today?

....

....

....

How I showed or received kindness today (others/self):

....

....

....

How I connected with nature today:

....

....

....

Something I did or said which took courage:

....

....

....

Who (which part of me) will show up tomorrow to make the day even better?

- Creator / Magician ☐
- Warrior / Courage ☐
- Leader / Inspiration ☐
- Love / Authentic Self ☐

....

....

....

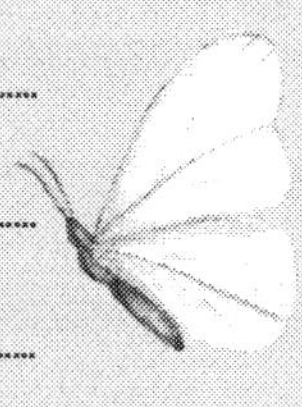

MORNING REFLECTION

My Power Word: " "Date:..................

Hmmm.... How I Feel Right Now Great

0 1 2 3 4 5 6 7 8 9 10

Today I'm grateful for:

....

....

....

My intention for the day:

....

....

....

A belief / habit to change:

....

....

....

What I can do today to get me closer to where I want to be tomorrow:

....

....

....

My daily affirmation:

....

....

....

EVENING REFLECTION

Date:..................

How I Feel Before Sleep

Hmmm.... Peaceful / Grateful

0 1 2 3 4 5 6 7 8 9 10

What did I learn today?

....

....

....

How I showed or received kindness today (others/self):

....

....

....

How I connected with nature today:

....

....

....

Something I did or said which took courage:

....

....

....

Who (which part of me) will show up tomorrow to make the day even better?

- Creator / Magician ☐
- Warrior / Courage ☐
- Leader / Inspiration ☐
- Love / Authentic Self ☐

....

....

....

MORNING REFLECTION

My Power Word: "   "Date:.................

Hmmm.... How I Feel Right Now Great

0 1 2 3 4 5 6 7 8 9 10

Today I'm grateful for:

....

....

....

My intention for the day:

....

....

....

A belief / habit to change:

....

....

....

What I can do today to get me closer to where I want to be tomorrow:

....

....

....

My daily affirmation:

....

....

....

EVENING REFLECTION

Date:..................

How I Feel Before Sleep

Hmmm.... Peaceful / Grateful

0 1 2 3 4 5 6 7 8 9 10

What did I learn today?

....

....

....

How I showed or received kindness today (others/self):

....

....

....

How I connected with nature today:

....

....

....

Something I did or said which took courage:

....

....

....

Who (which part of me) will show up tomorrow to make the day even better?

Creator / Magician ☐ ....

Warrior / Courage ☐ ....

Leader / Inspiration ☐ ....

Love / Authentic Self ☐

MORNING REFLECTION

My Power Word: " "Date:.................

Hmmm.... How I Feel Right Now Great

0 1 2 3 4 5 6 7 8 9 10

Today I'm grateful for:

....

....

....

My intention for the day:

....

....

....

A belief / habit to change:

....

....

....

What I can do today to get me closer to where I want to be tomorrow:

....

....

....

My daily affirmation:

....

....

....

EVENING REFLECTION

Date:..................

How I Feel Before Sleep

Hmmm.... 0 1 2 3 4 5 6 7 8 9 10 Peaceful / Grateful

What did I learn today?

....

....

....

How I showed or received kindness today (others/self):

....

....

....

How I connected with nature today:

....

....

....

Something I did or said which took courage:

....

....

....

Who (which part of me) will show up tomorrow to make the day even better?

Creator / Magician ☐ ....

Warrior / Courage ☐ ....

Leader / Inspiration ☐ ....

Love / Authentic Self ☐

MORNING REFLECTION

My Power Word: " " Date:..................

Hmmm.... How I Feel Right Now Great

0 1 2 3 4 5 6 7 8 9 10

Today I'm grateful for:

....

....

....

My intention for the day:

....

....

....

A belief / habit to change:

....

....

....

What I can do today to get me closer to where I want to be tomorrow:

....

....

....

My daily affirmation:

....

....

....

EVENING REFLECTION

Date:..................

How I Feel Before Sleep

Hmmm.... 0 1 2 3 4 5 6 7 8 9 10 Peaceful / Grateful

What did I learn today?

How I showed or received kindness today (others/self):

How I connected with nature today:

Something I did or said which took courage:

Who (which part of me) will show up tomorrow to make the day even better?

- Creator / Magician ☐
- Warrior / Courage ☐
- Leader / Inspiration ☐
- Love / Authentic Self ☐

MORNING REFLECTION

My Power Word: "   "Date:..................

Hmmm....   How I Feel Right Now   Great

0 1 2 3 4 5 6 7 8 9 10

Today I'm grateful for:

....

....

....

My intention for the day:

....

....

....

A belief / habit to change:

....

....

....

What I can do today to get me closer to where I want to be tomorrow:

....

....

....

My daily affirmation:

....

....

....

EVENING REFLECTION

Date:..................

How I Feel Before Sleep

Hmmm.... Peaceful / Grateful

0 1 2 3 4 5 6 7 8 9 10

What did I learn today?

....

....

....

How I showed or received kindness today (others/self):

....

....

....

How I connected with nature today:

....

....

....

Something I did or said which took courage:

....

....

....

Who (which part of me) will show up tomorrow to make the day even better?

- Creator / Magician ☐
- Warrior / Courage ☐
- Leader / Inspiration ☐
- Love / Authentic Self ☐

....

....

....

MORNING REFLECTION

My Power Word: " "Date:..................

Hmmm.... **How I Feel Right Now** Great

0 1 2 3 4 5 6 7 8 9 10

Today I'm grateful for:

My intention for the day:

A belief / habit to change:

What I can do today to get me closer to where I want to be tomorrow:

My daily affirmation:

EVENING REFLECTION

Date:..................

How I Feel Before Sleep

Hmmm.... Peaceful / Grateful

0 1 2 3 4 5 6 7 8 9 10

What did I learn today?

How I showed or received kindness today (others/self):

How I connected with nature today:

Something I did or said which took courage:

Who (which part of me) will show up tomorrow to make the day even better?

Creator / Magician

Warrior / Courage

Leader / Inspiration

Love / Authentic Self

bonus day

My Power Word: Date:

Mood/Emotion Tracker

○ ○ ○ ○ ○

SAD / LOW ⟷ HAPPY / ENERGISED

Space for Creativity

DOODLE, COLOUR, WORDS, THOUGHTS

I am Grateful for:

My Intention / Focus for today:

My Purpose / Mission:

What I GET to do today:

MORNING REFLECTION

My Power Word: "   "Date:..................

Hmmm....   How I Feel Right Now   Great

0 1 2 3 4 5 6 7 8 9 10

Today I'm grateful for:

....

....

....

My intention for the day:

....

....

....

A belief / habit to change:

....

....

....

What I can do today to get me closer to where I want to be tomorrow:

....

....

....

My daily affirmation:

....

....

....

EVENING REFLECTION

Date:..................

How I Feel Before Sleep

Hmmm.... 0 1 2 3 4 5 6 7 8 9 10 Peaceful / Grateful

What did I learn today?

....

....

....

How I showed or received kindness today (others/self):

....

....

....

How I connected with nature today:

....

....

....

Something I did or said which took courage:

....

....

....

Who (which part of me) will show up tomorrow to make the day even better?

- Creator / Magician ☐
- Warrior / Courage ☐
- Leader / Inspiration ☐
- Love / Authentic Self ☐

....

....

....

MORNING REFLECTION

My Power Word: " "Date:..................

Hmmm.... **How I Feel Right Now** Great

0 1 2 3 4 5 6 7 8 9 10

Today I'm grateful for:

My intention for the day:

A belief / habit to change:

What I can do today to get me closer to where I want to be tomorrow:

My daily affirmation:

EVENING REFLECTION

Date:..................

How I Feel Before Sleep

Hmmm.... Peaceful / Grateful

0 1 2 3 4 5 6 7 8 9 10

What did I learn today?

How I showed or received kindness today (others/self):

How I connected with nature today:

Something I did or said which took courage:

Who (which part of me) will show up tomorrow to make the day even better?

Creator / Magician ☐

Warrior / Courage ☐

Leader / Inspiration ☐

Love / Authentic Self ☐

MORNING REFLECTION

My Power Word: " **" Date:.................**

Hmmm.... **How I Feel Right Now** Great

0 1 2 3 4 5 6 7 8 9 10

Today I'm grateful for:

....

....

....

My intention for the day:

....

....

....

A belief / habit to change:

....

....

....

What I can do today to get me closer to where I want to be tomorrow:

....

....

....

My daily affirmation:

....

....

....

EVENING REFLECTION

Date:.................

How I Feel Before Sleep

Hmmm.... Peaceful / Grateful

0 1 2 3 4 5 6 7 8 9 10

What did I learn today?

....

....

....

How I showed or received kindness today (others/self):

....

....

....

How I connected with nature today:

....

....

....

Something I did or said which took courage:

....

....

....

Who (which part of me) will show up tomorrow to make the day even better?

- Creator / Magician ☐
- Warrior / Courage ☐
- Leader / Inspiration ☐
- Love / Authentic Self ☐

....

....

....

MORNING REFLECTION

My Power Word: " "Date:.................

Hmmm.... How I Feel Right Now Great

0 1 2 3 4 5 6 7 8 9 10

Today I'm grateful for:

....

....

....

My intention for the day:

....

....

....

A belief / habit to change:

....

....

....

What I can do today to get me closer to where I want to be tomorrow:

....

....

....

My daily affirmation:

....

....

....

EVENING REFLECTION

Date:..................

How I Feel Before Sleep

Hmmm.... Peaceful / Grateful

0 1 2 3 4 5 6 7 8 9 10

What did I learn today?

....

....

....

How I showed or received kindness today (others/self):

....

....

....

How I connected with nature today:

....

....

....

Something I did or said which took courage:

....

....

....

Who (which part of me) will show up tomorrow to make the day even better?

- [ ] Creator / Magician
- [ ] Warrior / Courage
- [ ] Leader / Inspiration
- [ ] Love / Authentic Self

....

....

....

MORNING REFLECTION

My Power Word: " "Date:..................

Hmmm.... How I Feel Right Now Great

0 1 2 3 4 5 6 7 8 9 10

Today I'm grateful for:

....

....

....

My intention for the day:

....

....

....

A belief / habit to change:

....

....

....

What I can do today to get me closer to where I want to be tomorrow:

....

....

....

My daily affirmation:

....

....

....

EVENING REFLECTION

Date:..................

How I Feel Before Sleep

Hmmm.... Peaceful / Grateful

0 1 2 3 4 5 6 7 8 9 10

What did I learn today?

....

....

....

How I showed or received kindness today (others/self):

....

....

....

How I connected with nature today:

....

....

....

Something I did or said which took courage:

....

....

....

Who (which part of me) will show up tomorrow to make the day even better?

- Creator / Magician ☐
- Warrior / Courage ☐
- Leader / Inspiration ☐
- Love / Authentic Self ☐

....

....

....

MORNING REFLECTION

My Power Word: " "Date:..................

Hmmm.... **How I Feel Right Now** Great

0 1 2 3 4 5 6 7 8 9 10

Today I'm grateful for:

....

....

....

My intention for the day:

....

....

....

A belief / habit to change:

....

....

....

What I can do today to get me closer to where I want to be tomorrow:

....

....

....

My daily affirmation:

....

....

....

EVENING REFLECTION

Date:..................

How I Feel Before Sleep

Hmmm.... Peaceful / Grateful

0 1 2 3 4 5 6 7 8 9 10

What did I learn today?

....

....

....

How I showed or received kindness today (others/self):

....

....

....

How I connected with nature today:

....

....

....

Something I did or said which took courage:

....

....

....

Who (which part of me) will show up tomorrow to make the day even better?

- Creator / Magician ☐
- Warrior / Courage ☐
- Leader / Inspiration ☐
- Love / Authentic Self ☐

....

....

....

MORNING REFLECTION

My Power Word: "   "Date:..................

Hmmm....   How I Feel Right Now   Great

0 1 2 3 4 5 6 7 8 9 10

Today I'm grateful for:

....

....

....

My intention for the day:

....

....

....

A belief / habit to change:

....

....

....

What I can do today to get me closer to where I want to be tomorrow:

....

....

....

My daily affirmation:

....

....

....

EVENING REFLECTION

Date:.................

How I Feel Before Sleep

Hmmm.... Peaceful / Grateful

0 1 2 3 4 5 6 7 8 9 10

What did I learn today?

How I showed or received kindness today (others/self):

How I connected with nature today:

Something I did or said which took courage:

Who (which part of me) will show up tomorrow to make the day even better?

Creator / Magician ☐

Warrior / Courage ☐

Leader / Inspiration ☐

Love / Authentic Self ☐

MORNING REFLECTION

My Power Word: "   " Date:..................

Hmmm....   How I Feel Right Now   Great

0 1 2 3 4 5 6 7 8 9 10

Today I'm grateful for:

...

...

...

My intention for the day:

...

...

...

A belief / habit to change:

...

...

...

What I can do today to get me closer to where I want to be tomorrow:

...

...

...

My daily affirmation:

...

...

...

EVENING REFLECTION

Date:..................

How I Feel Before Sleep

Hmmm.... Peaceful / Grateful

0 1 2 3 4 5 6 7 8 9 10

What did I learn today?

How I showed or received kindness today (others/self):

How I connected with nature today:

Something I did or said which took courage:

Who (which part of me) will show up tomorrow to make the day even better?

- Creator / Magician ☐
- Warrior / Courage ☐
- Leader / Inspiration ☐
- Love / Authentic Self ☐

MORNING REFLECTION

My Power Word: " "Date:..................

Hmmm.... How I Feel Right Now Great

0 1 2 3 4 5 6 7 8 9 10

Today I'm grateful for:

My intention for the day:

A belief / habit to change:

What I can do today to get me closer to where I want to be tomorrow:

My daily affirmation:

EVENING REFLECTION

Date:.................

How I Feel Before Sleep

Hmmm.... Peaceful / Grateful

0 1 2 3 4 5 6 7 8 9 10

What did I learn today?

....

....

....

How I showed or received kindness today (others/self):

....

....

....

How I connected with nature today:

....

....

....

Something I did or said which took courage:

....

....

....

Who (which part of me) will show up tomorrow to make the day even better?

- [ ] Creator / Magician
- [ ] Warrior / Courage
- [ ] Leader / Inspiration
- [ ] Love / Authentic Self

....

....

....

MORNING REFLECTION

My Power Word: " " Date:..................

Hmmm.... **How I Feel Right Now** Great

0 1 2 3 4 5 6 7 8 9 10

Today I'm grateful for:

....

....

....

My intention for the day:

....

....

....

A belief / habit to change:

....

....

....

What I can do today to get me closer to where I want to be tomorrow:

....

....

....

My daily affirmation:

....

....

....

EVENING REFLECTION

Date:..................

How I Feel Before Sleep

Hmmm.... Peaceful / Grateful

0 1 2 3 4 5 6 7 8 9 10

What did I learn today?

....

....

....

How I showed or received kindness today (others/self):

....

....

....

How I connected with nature today:

....

....

....

Something I did or said which took courage:

....

....

....

Who (which part of me) will show up tomorrow to make the day even better?

Creator / Magician ☐

Warrior / Courage ☐

Leader / Inspiration ☐

Love / Authentic Self ☐

....

....

....

MORNING REFLECTION

My Power Word: "   "Date:..................

Hmmm....   How I Feel Right Now   Great

0 1 2 3 4 5 6 7 8 9 10

Today I'm grateful for:

....

....

....

My intention for the day:

....

....

....

A belief / habit to change:

....

....

....

What I can do today to get me closer to where I want to be tomorrow:

....

....

....

My daily affirmation:

....

....

....

EVENING REFLECTION

Date:..................

How I Feel Before Sleep

Hmmm.... Peaceful / Grateful

0 1 2 3 4 5 6 7 8 9 10

What did I learn today?

....

....

....

How I showed or received kindness today (others/self):

....

....

....

How I connected with nature today:

....

....

....

Something I did or said which took courage:

....

....

....

Who (which part of me) will show up tomorrow to make the day even better?

- Creator / Magician ☐
- Warrior / Courage ☐
- Leader / Inspiration ☐
- Love / Authentic Self ☐

....

....

....

bonus day

My Power Word:

Date:

Mood/Emotion Tracker

○ ○ ○ ○ ○

SAD / LOW ⟷ HAPPY / ENERGISED

Space for Creativity

DOODLE, COLOUR, WORDS, THOUGHTS

I am Grateful for:

My Intention / Focus for today:

My Purpose / Mission:

What I GET to do today:

my notes

my notes

Love of Some Sort

As I Love myself, Some kind of Love is calling me.
The kind I have never felt.

But where can I find this Love that I seek?
Well... Why does your heart ever decide to beat?

It beats for someone who meets your eye,
Never forgetting the feeling inside.
It beats to be held, it beats to be listened, it beats to be tended, and sometimes mended.
It beats for warmth, it beats for belonging, it beats for connection: An antidote to your longing.

For your soul hides a place not everyone can find.
But someday it may be fully recognised.

So I hope you see Love everywhere you look and somehow you'll know you were never really stuck!

You are always on your way.
So a little trust in each day and know that the beat of your heart has its own rhythm, it's own sound.

Let it be yours, so you can be found.

Poem by
Deirdre Whitmore

© copyright Deirdre Whitmore 2024

Congratulations!

You did it!

You have completed your journal for several months practising gratitude, healing and empowerment.

A beautiful and beneficial new habit you have created and that's worth celebrating!

I'd love to hear from you about how the journal has changed, improved or transformed your life.

Email linzi@linzimeaden.com or leave a kind review online where you purchased this.

And there's no time like the present to gift yourself (and friends / family / colleagues) with another new copy of this journal (or one of my others) to continue reaping the benefits for longer.

Thank you for being YOU and for taking ownership for your life.

With love & gratitude,
Linzi x

About The Creator

Linzi Meaden is a Clinical Hypnotherapist, Trauma Therapist, and Mental Health Advocate.

She runs a private clinic in Tunbridge Wells, UK.

Having lost her only sibling to suicide during the pandemic in 2020, Linzi has made it her mission to raise more awareness about the importance of expressing our emotions and learning how to embrace life despite adversity.

Through her work, Linzi inspires others to prioritise mental health and live authentically with courage and purpose.

In addition to her clinical practice, she extends her impact by sharing her story as the author of *What Suicide Left Behind*, hosting a support group for *Suicide Loss Survivors*, founding *The Souls of Courage Club* with online programmes, and serving as an Ambassador for various charities.

Printed in Great Britain
by Amazon

9b830a6c-3631-4192-9e09-7109d57984a6R01